ANXIOUS, AVOIDANT, & DISORGANIZED ATTACHMENT RECOVERY

WORKBOOK

BOOKS BY LULU NICHOLSON

Transformative Shadow Work: Guide, Workbook & Journal—The 3-Step System to Embrace Your Hidden Self and Transcend Emotional Triggers & Past Traumas to Reduce Stress, Enhance Personal Growth, and Improve Relationships

Codependency Recovery Workbook: Step-by-Step Guide to Overcome Fear of Abandonment, Set Strong Boundaries, and Develop Healthy Relationships by Restoring Self-Worth & Self-Love

ANXIOUS, AVOIDANT, & DISORGANIZED ATTACHMENT RECOVERY

WORKBOOK

APPLY **ATTACHMENT THEORY** TO UNDERSTAND YOUR BEHAVIOR PATTERNS, IMPROVE EMOTIONAL REGULATION, AND BUILD SECURE & HEALTHY RELATIONSHIPS

LULU NICHOLSON

© Copyright **Lulu Nicholson 2024 - All rights reserved.**

The content within this book may not be reproduced, duplicated, or transmitted without direct written permission from the author or the publisher.

Under no circumstances will any blame or legal responsibility be held against the publisher or author for any damages, reparation, or monetary loss due to the information contained within this book. Either directly or indirectly. You are responsible for your own choices, actions, and results.

Legal Notice:

This book is copyright-protected. This book is only for personal use. You cannot amend, distribute, sell, use, quote, or paraphrase any part of the content within this book without the author's or publisher's consent.

Disclaimer Notice:

Please note that the information contained within this document is for educational and entertainment purposes only. All efforts have been made to present accurate, up-to-date, reliable, and complete information. No warranties of any kind are declared or implied. Readers acknowledge that the author is not engaging in rendering legal, financial, medical, or professional advice. The content within this book has been derived from various sources. Please consult a licensed professional before attempting any techniques outlined in this book.

By reading this document, the reader agrees that under no circumstances is the author responsible for any losses, direct or indirect, which are incurred as a result of the use of the information contained within this document, including, but not limited to, — errors, omissions, or inaccuracies.

Contents

Introduction (1)

01.
Beyond Labels—Understanding the Depths of Attachment Styles

Defining Anxious, Avoidant, and Disorganized Attachment Styles (4)
The Influence of Past Experiences (6)
Insecure Attachment Styles and Their Origins (7)
The Influence of Early Childhood Attachment (8)
Understanding Secure Attachment in Relationships (9)
The Dark Side of Labeling (10)
Understanding Adaptive Responses Within Each Style (12)
Identifying Hidden Attachment Styles in Others (15)
Quiz: Discover Your Attachment Style in Different Contexts (18)

02.
The Role of Attachment in Relationships

The Influence of Attachment on Self-Perception and Internal Dialogue (21)
Manifestations of Attachment in the Workplace (24)
Navigating Friendships Through an Attachment Lens (27)
Attachment Styles and Romantic Attraction (30)
Exercise: Self-Compassion Journaling Prompts (35)

03.

Emotional Archaeology—Excavating the Impact of Early Experiences

Mapping the Influence of Childhood Experiences on Adult Attachments (40)

Addressing Generational Trauma and Its Role in Creating Attachment Issues (42)

Techniques to Reshape Childhood Narratives for Healing (45)

Reparenting Yourself as a Tool for Secure Attachments (48)

Exercise: Family Attachment Map for Generational Insights (50)

04.

Emotional Alchemy—Turning Attachment-Driven Reactions into Conscious Responses

Understanding the Link Between Attachment Styles and Nervous System Responses (55)

Tailored Emotional Regulation Techniques for Different Attachments (57)

Practicing Emotional Flexibility to Cultivate Thoughtful Responses (61)

Exercise: Pause-and-Reflect (65)

05.

Building Secure Relationships in a World of Insecure Patterns

Characteristics of Secure Attachment Behaviors (68)

Building Trust with Anxious and Avoidant Partners (75)

Breaking Toxic Cycles and Understanding Security as a Process (78)

Exercise: Relationship Audit for Assessing Security Levels (81)

06.

Mastering the Art of Boundaries without Losing Connection

Transforming Boundaries from Barriers to Protective Filters (87)

Setting Compassionate Yet Firm Boundaries with Loved Ones (89)

Role-Playing Exercises for Practicing Boundary Reinforcement (93)

Exercise: Scripts for Expressing Boundary Needs Effectively (96)

07.
Beyond Communication—Creating Emotional Safety
Differentiating Between Communication and Emotional Safety (101)
Developing Emotional Attunement for Deeper Connections (103)
Prioritizing Emotional Resilience in All Interactions (105)
Exercise: Strengthening Rapport Through Consistent Emotional Presence (108)

08.
Your Ongoing Journey to Secure Attachment
Encouraging Ongoing Development of Secure Relationships (110)
Highlighting the Significance of Introspection and Curiosity (112)
Making Room for Setbacks in Your Relationships (113)
Final Reflection on Setting Goals in Various Relationships (135)
Commitment to Adaptability in Evolving Attachments (117)
Exercise: Setting Healthy Relationship Values and Goals (119)

Conclusion (123)
References (127)

Special Gifts to My Readers

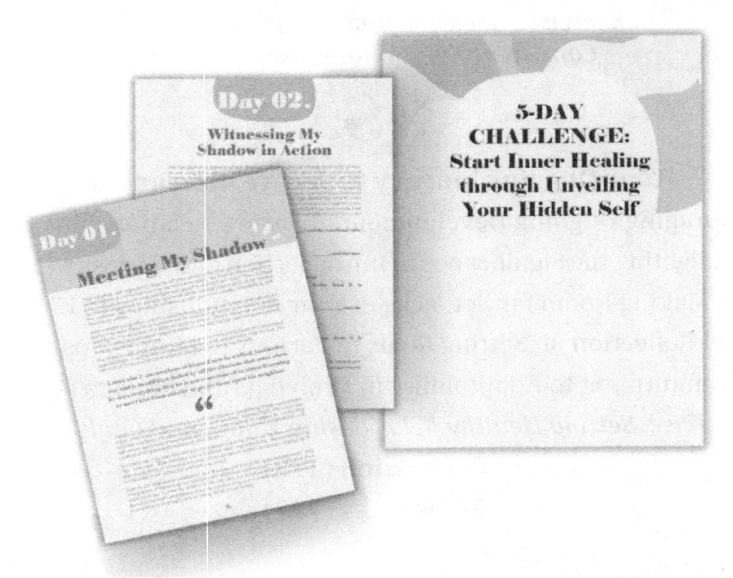

Start Inner Healing Through Unveiling Your Hidden Self.'

Simply scan the QR code and provide the email address you'd like it delivered to. This 5-day program will help you begin your self-improvement journey on the right foot:

Day 1: MEETING MY SHADOW

Day 2: WITNESSING MY SHADOW IN ACTION

Day 3: INTEGRATING MY SHADOW

Day 4: ACCEPTING MY SHADOW

Day 5: BECOMING WHOLE

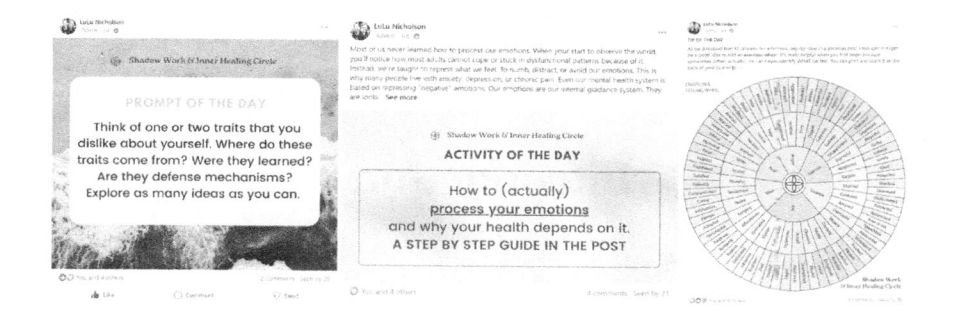

Additionally, I invite you to join the
'Shadow Work & Inner Healing Circle' Facebook Group
for Daily Prompts and Activities.

This new community is designed for beginners and those well into their journey, and it is suitable for:

- Anyone seeking to incorporate inner work into their daily routine and make it a lifelong practice.
- Anyone in search of support and accountability within a private, safe space.
- Anyone looking to connect with like-minded individuals.
- Anyone seeking tangible, practical steps and healing tools to delve deeper into their journey.
- Anyone (and I mean anyone) seeking to create change in their life!

00.

Introduction

One of the best guides to how to be self-loving is to give ourselves the love we are often dreaming about receiving from others. –Bell Hooks

>

The Ties That Shape Us

Understanding the dynamics of human relationships can feel like navigating a maze without a map. Whether we're caught in the orbit of romantic partnerships, enduring the ups and downs of family connections, or blending into the workplace with colleagues, our attachment styles are quietly at play behind the scenes. These patterns shape how we connect, communicate, and cope with those around us, often echoing the past experiences that formed them.

Think about the relationship between you and your closest friend—the special bond you share does in some way mirror the dynamics of your childhood attachments, such as your relationship with your early childhood friends. Or consider your professional environment: Have you ever noticed a colleague whose presence reminds you of a childhood caregiver or school teacher, inexplicably stirring feelings of inadequacy or self-doubt? These echoes from our emotional history resonate across various aspects of life, subtly influencing our daily interactions. It's easy to overlook these undercurrents, convincing ourselves they are mere coincidences or unrelated quirks. However, uncovering the secret language of attachment offers a chance to decode these experiences.

Every relationship in your life teaches you something profound about your own patterns and responses. This book isn't about reopening old wounds and dwelling on where you've been; it's about envisioning where you can go by analyzing your interactions with others and reflecting on how you can make your relationships feel safer and more fulfilling. It's an evolving adventure where understanding oneself becomes a lifelong mission, allowing you to better understand others and creating rich opportunities for personal transformation and healing.

What Is Attachment Theory?

Throughout the book, you will be taught different aspects of attachment theory to better understand your relationship patterns and behaviors. This theory was discovered by psychologist John Bowlby and later expanded by psychologist Mary Ainsworth (Cherry, 2023). It seeks to explain the fragile attachment between a child and caregiver (usually their mother), which sets the tone for the child's sense of safety and ability to build healthy and trusting relationships later in life.

Unfortunately, we don't get to choose our attachment styles, since our circumstances and environments shape how we relate to others. Nevertheless, learning about our attachment history allows us to confront maladaptive relationship patterns that stem from fear-based and insecure coping behaviors we adopted as children. What makes this book unique is that we explore not only our attachment styles but those of our loved ones too, which can help us become more aware, empathetic, and responsive to their needs. Moreover, we will discuss how attachment styles are not fixed and that sometimes we might exhibit qualities of more than one attachment style, depending on our contextual experiences.

The Value of This Book

Through interactive elements such as prebook reflection exercises, you will be actively engaged from the onset and encouraged to confront the emotional complexities you find in your current relationships. These exercises serve as guideposts, directing your exploration inward and laying the groundwork for the transformative process ahead.

INTRODUCTION

As you turn each page, you're invited to peel back layers—much like the unfolding skins of an onion. Within these pages lies the potential to gain deeper insights into yourself and others. Imagine the possibilities of forming more genuine, resilient, and fulfilling connections. As your understanding of attachment broadens, so too does your capacity to foster healthier relationships.

Consider this introduction an open invitation to go deeper into the multifaceted world of attachment theory. It's a path laden with discoveries waiting to be made, offering new perspectives on how you perceive your own identity and how you interact with the people who walk through your life.

Throughout this book, you'll find stories from individuals who, much like you, have encountered the benefits of understanding their attachment styles. Their journeys underscore the universal themes within us all—the desire for connection, the fear of abandonment, and the quest for authentic relationships unmarred by past insecurities.

When faced with life's challenges, relationships can either present a comforting haven or a source of discord and pain. Recognizing and understanding attachment styles equips you with the tools to navigate this delicate balance. By embracing the journey of discovery outlined in this book, you grant yourself permission to evolve beyond entrenched patterns, emerging with a renewed sense of self-direction and purpose.

Prepare to embark on a transformative quest—one that is sure to enrich not only your understanding of human connections but also the relationship you maintain with yourself. Let's step into this expedition together, one chapter at a time, guided by the currents of insight and knowledge.

01.

Beyond Labels—Understanding the Depths of Attachment Styles

Attachment principles teach us that most people are only as needy as their unmet needs. –Amir Levine

❝

Defining Anxious, Avoidant, and Disorganized Attachment Styles

Understanding attachment styles involves more than just putting people into simple categories. It is important to consider how our early environments shape our behaviors. Attachment styles can include terms like anxious, avoidant, or disorganized, but these labels are only the beginning. The real focus should be on how these attachment patterns appear in our daily lives and relationships. This approach requires us to dig deeper into the ways these styles affect our connections with other people.

The bonds we create with our caregivers during childhood have a lasting impact on our adult relationships. For example, a child who feels secure and loved will likely develop confidence in forming relationships as they grow older. This sense of security can lead to healthy communication and trust in future connections. On the other hand, a child who experiences neglect or inconsistency in caregiving might struggle with anxiety in relationships, feeling unsure whether they can rely on others.

We also need to consider the different ways children react to their caregivers. Some may cling to their caregivers, feeling anxious whenever they are apart. Others might push away, displaying avoidant behaviors by avoiding close relationships. Understanding these dynamics helps us see how our childhood influences the way we interact with friends, family, and romantic partners later in life.

Awareness of our attachment styles can also help us avoid repeating past mistakes. For instance, if someone recognizes that they always pick partners who are emotionally unavailable, they can take steps to change this pattern. This might mean taking a break from dating to reflect on what they truly want in a partner or seeking relationships with people who show consistent emotional availability.

Being logged into your own attachment style allows you to identify triggers that cause you to react in certain ways. A moment of anger or jealousy often comes from deep-seated fears linked to our attachment history. Knowing this can help you manage your responses more effectively. Instead of jumping to conclusions or acting out, you may try calming techniques, like deep breathing or taking time to think before reacting.

Over time, you can reevaluate your relationships based on your understanding of attachment styles. This assessment might lead you to distance yourself from relationships that don't serve your emotional needs. For example, you may need to reconsider a friendship that feels overly demanding or emotionally intensive, realizing that protecting your own emotional space is necessary for your well-being.

At the same time, pursuing healthier relationships might encourage you to embrace more vulnerability. Feeling secure in a relationship can lead you to open up more than you previously would have, enhancing emotional depth and connection in your relationships. Such transformations are often gradual as you learn to trust in healthy relationships and gain confidence in your ability to maintain boundaries.

The Influence of Past Experiences

Your attachment styles are shaped significantly by your past experiences. These early events, especially during childhood, can set the tone for how you interact with others as an adult. One common example is growing up in a family that experienced a divorce. This situation can amount to a substantial emotional shift for you as a child. You might have observed the disintegration of your parents' relationship, leading to confusion and feelings of abandonment. Such experiences could have created a lasting impact, influencing how you perceive relationships in your adulthood.

When children witness their parents' separation, they often internalize certain beliefs about love and commitment. For instance, you might start to think that all relationships are temporary and that it's safer to keep emotional distance. This belief can lead to you exhibiting avoidant behaviors in your relationships. You might shy away from deep emotional connections, fearing that these connections might also break apart. This pattern can become a cycle, where you struggle to settle into lasting relationships because you are constantly worried about being hurt like you were in your formative years.

To change this course, it is essential to recognize their origins. Acknowledging that past experiences influence present behavior can be the first step toward healing. Often, this involves introspection and possibly even seeking professional help to understand these patterns better. Therapy can provide a safe space to explore these feelings and beliefs. For instance, a therapist might help you identify how your childhood experiences are shaping your current reactions to intimacy and relationships.

As you start to unravel these narratives, you can begin to challenge your relationship beliefs, asking yourself thought-provoking questions like, "Is it really true that all relationships end?" or, "Can I allow myself to connect with others without fear?" Such questioning can lead to a more balanced perspective. It's essential to realize that not every relationship will mirror your past. To ingrain empowering beliefs about relationships in your mind, a practical approach could be to start small by opening up to your friends or loved ones about your bonding experiences as a child before moving toward romantic connections.

CHAPTER 1

Insecure Attachment Styles and Their Origins

Insecure attachment styles are characterized by a lack of trust and intimacy in relationships, often leading to feelings of anxiety or avoidance. These styles typically develop in early childhood due to inconsistent or negative experiences with caregivers. When a child's emotional needs are not consistently met—whether through neglect, inconsistency, or overprotectiveness—they may form a sense of insecurity that impacts their future relationships. There are three main types of insecure attachment styles: anxious, avoidant, and disorganized. Below is an overview of how they can manifest in a child's life.

Anxious Attachment

Anxious attachment is identified by its origins in inconsistent caregiving, which creates an underlying sense of uncertainty in individuals (Cherry, 2023). Caregivers who are sometimes responsive and at other times not can lead children to become hyper-attuned to emotional cues. This heightened sensitivity results in an acute fear of abandonment, as individuals constantly seek reassurance that they are loved and valued.

The unpredictability of the caregiver's behavior instills a deep-seated anxiety, compelling those with anxious attachment to develop clingy behaviors in relationships. They may find themselves preoccupied with the possibility of rejection, interpreting even benign actions from their partner as potential signs of disinterest. Such individuals often derive self-worth from their ability to secure and maintain relational bonds, fearing that any lapse might result in loss (Cherry, 2023).

Avoidant Attachment

On the other side of the spectrum is avoidant attachment. This style takes root when caregivers are overly protective or dismissive, prompting a child to prioritize independence over emotional intimacy (Cherry, 2023). These caregivers might provide for physical necessities but neglect the child's emotional needs, signaling to the child that vulnerability is either dangerous or fruitless. As a result, those with avoidant attachment learn to suppress their emotional expressions, viewing reliance on others as a liability. They grow up valuing self-reliance, often keeping others at arm's length to preserve their autonomy.

Intimacy, therefore, becomes challenging, as they struggle to open up and trust deeply. Relationships might progress smoothly until deeper emotional connections are required, at which point the avoidantly attached individual might retreat, leaving partners feeling isolated and confused about the sudden emotional withdrawal.

Disorganized Attachment

Disorganized attachment is perhaps the most complex, stemming from environments characterized by trauma and inconsistency. This style reflects a blend of internal conflict, where the source of safety (the caregiver) is also a source of fear or distress (Cherry, 2023). In such scenarios, children experience conflicting emotions—wanting to approach their caregiver for comfort while simultaneously fearing them due to unpredictable or frightening behaviors.

This fluctuation leads to erratic relationship patterns as adults. Trust becomes a significant challenge; those with disorganized attachment often oscillate between intense closeness and abrupt detachment. Their early experiences disrupt their ability to regulate emotions effectively, causing inner turmoil that manifests in bewildering relational behaviors. They might crave connection yet anticipate betrayal, which is confusing both for themselves and their partners.

The Influence of Early Childhood Attachments

But why do these early experiences hold so much sway over adult relationships? Attachment theory, largely developed by John Bowlby, posits that these patterns are survival strategies developed during early childhood (Cherry, 2023). By understanding these styles, adults can better understand the roots of their relationship struggles and work toward healthier dynamics.

Growing up, children adapt to the environment set by their caregivers, forming expectations about how relationships work based on this model. Anxious individuals, through persistent seeking of validation, essentially attempt to prevent the rejection experienced in childhood. Conversely, those with avoidant tendencies strive to protect themselves from anticipated emotional neglect.

Awareness of attachment styles allows for transformation. For example, someone recognizing their anxious tendencies might begin to understand the importance of self-soothing techniques and communication in relationships. Recognizing avoidant traits could lead one to gradually build tolerance for vulnerability, realizing it doesn't equate to loss of independence but rather enhances relational depth. For those navigating disorganized attachment, therapy often provides a vital avenue for reconstructing trust and stability.

In acknowledging that these attachment styles are not rigid labels, but dynamic behaviors shaped by past caregiving environments, there's room for growth and healing. With awareness and effort, individuals can adjust their tendencies, moving toward more secure attachment patterns.

Understanding Secure Attachment in Relationships

Securely attached individuals are often seen as confident in their relationships. This confidence comes from their early experiences with consistent caregiving (Cherry, 2023). When a child grows up with caregivers who respond to their needs reliably, they learn that they can trust others. For example, if a child cries and their caregiver comes to provide comfort, the child develops a sense of security. This sense of security shapes their view of relationships in adulthood.

Consistent caregiving plays a critical role in forming secure attachment. This means that caregivers must be available and responsive to a child's needs most of the time. A stable environment, where the child feels safe and valued, allows them to explore their world while knowing they have a secure base to return to when they need support.

Children who experience consistent caregiving are likely to develop a sense of worth that shapes their interpersonal connections. They often expect others to respond to their needs as their caregivers did. This expectation can lead them to form healthy and strong bonds in adulthood. In practical terms, when someone enters a romantic relationship, for example, a securely attached individual is more likely to communicate their feelings openly. They trust that their partner will listen and understand, leading to more meaningful and fulfilling connections. This quality can strengthen the relationship and deepen emotional intimacy.

Moreover, people with secure attachments also tend to cope with stress more effectively. They usually perceive challenges as manageable because they have a solid support system. For instance, if they face a stressful situation at work or in their personal life, they are likely to seek support from their partner or friends without fear of rejection. They believe in their ability to navigate problems, whether big or small, because they trust in the relationships they have built. This resilience contributes to a more balanced emotional state overall.

The Dark Side of Labeling

In today's world, labels often act as shorthand for complex behaviors and traits. While they can provide quick insights into one's experiences, reliance on these labels risks oversimplifying nuanced human behaviors. Attachment styles, like anxious or avoidant, are good examples of how such labels can obscure the complexities of individual personalities.

By using labels, we risk ignoring unique variations that arise from personal experiences. Contextual factors play a significant role in shaping our behaviors, yet these are often missed when we rely solely on generalized descriptors. For instance, two people with an anxious attachment style might demonstrate vastly different behaviors based on their upbringing, culture, or life experiences. By placing them under one umbrella term, we may lose sight of these crucial differences.

Moreover, attachment styles do not remain static. They are influenced by experiences and evolve across relationships and time. This dynamic nature is often overlooked when we focus on static labels. A person with a predominantly avoidant style, for example, may develop more secure traits as they engage in healthy, supportive relationships. Alternatively, they may have one or two relationships with a close friend or partner where they display secure relational patterns, despite being avoidant with other people who aren't as close to them.

It's therefore important to view attachment styles loosely, seeing them more as a guideline to raise awareness of your unconscious relationship patterns rather than a fixed aspect of your identity— the latter unintentionally boxing you into a category that you don't display all the time. Understanding that attachment styles are part of a fluid spectrum allows room for a more holistic view of who you are and the quality of your relationships.

Misinterpretations of attachment styles can have significant implications for personal growth and relational dynamics. If someone identifies too strongly with a particular label, it could serve as a self-fulfilling prophecy, limiting their potential for change and development. For example, if a person believes they are inherently disorganized in relationships due to past trauma, they might feel resigned to this fate, hindering progress toward healthier relationship practices.

The impact of misconceptions extends beyond the individual, affecting interpersonal connections and expectations. When partners, friends, or family members perceive someone's behavior through the lens of a simplistic label, it can lead to misunderstandings and strained relationships. Recognizing that behaviors attributed to attachment styles are part of a broader context helps cultivate empathy and patience in interactions.

By consciously moving beyond labels, we open ourselves to a greater appreciation of human complexity. This awareness invites us to embrace diversity in emotional expression and interaction, encouraging personal reflection and adaptation. The journey of examining our attachment styles and those of others is one of continuous learning and self-discovery.

Genuine connection requires us to pay attention to the subtleties of our own and others' behaviors, adjusting our perceptions and responses accordingly. This practice, while challenging, promotes stronger, more resilient relationships. It empowers us to approach interactions with curiosity rather than judgment, creating environments where all attachment styles can coexist harmoniously.

In pursuit of healthier relationships, it is vital to acknowledge the evolving nature of attachment styles as integral components of our identity. Moving away from restrictive labels helps dismantle preconceived notions and cultivates a deeper acceptance of ourselves and others. Through adopting this perspective, every relational challenge becomes an opportunity for growth and transformation.

Understanding Adaptive Responses Within Each Style

Understanding adaptive responses is crucial in recognizing how individuals react differently to various situations. Each person has a unique style that influences their responses, making it important to explore these styles in depth. By doing so, we can develop a better understanding of ourselves and others.

Adaptive responses are the ways people adjust their behavior and thinking patterns in response to external challenges or stimuli. These responses can vary widely based on a person's temperament, past experiences, and emotional state. For example, someone who faces a stressful work environment may adapt by becoming more organized and focused, while another may retreat into avoidance behaviors. By recognizing these differences, we can begin to see how our styles impact our lives and relationships.

CHAPTER 1

Adaptive Features of Anxious Attachment

As we have discussed earlier, anxious attachment is an instinctual behavior rooted deeply in the need for survival. This style manifests through a persistent emphasis on maintaining connections with others, often driven by fear of abandonment. Imagine a child whose caregivers were inconsistently responsive. This unpredictability can lead the child to become hypervigilant, constantly seeking reassurance from those around them. As adults, such individuals might find themselves overly sensitive to changes in relationships, fearing the loss of bonds that symbolize security. They may experience an ongoing loop of seeking closeness and reassurance, believing these efforts will secure the connection they desperately crave.

Adaptive Features of Avoidant Attachment

Avoidant attachment, on the other hand, highlights a different type of adaptation. It revolves around the development of self-preservation and independence, especially prevalent in environments where emotional needs are disregarded or met with turbulence. For a child growing up in such settings, expressing emotions or relying on others might have felt futile or dangerous. As a result, avoidantly attached individuals often learn to rely on themselves, sealing off their vulnerability to protect against potential pain or disappointment. In adult relationships, this can manifest as a reluctance to depend on others or express personal feelings, favoring autonomy over intimacy.

Adaptive Features of Disorganized Attachment

Disorganized attachment presents a complex interplay of behaviors, evolved as a reaction to unpredictable and sometimes traumatic early experiences. This style lacks coherence, often blending anxious and avoidant tendencies, reflecting a history marked by chaos. Children who grew up with disorganized attachment might have experienced caregivers as both protectors and sources of fear.

Picture a child whose caregiver alternates between nurturing and threatening behaviors. The child learns to respond with confusion, never quite sure what to expect next. As these children grow into adulthood, they might struggle to trust others fully, swaying between a desire for connection and an impulse to withdraw.

Understanding that these attachment styles are adaptive strategies can be transformative. Recognizing them as responses rather than fixed traits allows individuals to approach their patterns with compassion. For instance, someone with an anxious attachment style might learn to recognize their drive for reassurance as a learned response to earlier inconsistencies. Instead of viewing this tendency as a flaw, it can become an opportunity for self-growth and healing.

Similarly, by acknowledging their desire for independence, individuals with avoidant attachment can explore safe ways of expressing vulnerability without feeling compromised. This awareness creates pathways for deeper, more fulfilling connections, challenging the belief that self-reliance must always equate to emotional distance. For those with disorganized attachment, understanding their often contradictory behaviors as outcomes of past unpredictability opens up avenues for healing. They can begin to develop strategies that allow them to navigate relationships with greater predictability, fostering stability that supports inner peace.

A crucial aspect of working with attachment styles is developing self-regulation skills. By identifying one's unique attachment-driven behaviors, individuals can cultivate skills to manage emotional responses that align more closely with their authentic selves. This process involves self-reflection and sometimes therapeutic intervention, which encourages exploration and resolution of deep-rooted fears and expectations.

Engaging with these adaptive behaviors requires patience and vulnerability, both within oneself and in relationships with others. It's about recognizing patterns, understanding origins, and incrementally shifting toward healthier expressions of attachment. Compassionate self-inquiry and openness to change are key components, which allow individuals to reshape how they perceive and engage with their relational worlds.

CHAPTER 1

Identifying Hidden Attachment Styles in Others

Understanding the attachment styles of others is essential for strengthening your relationships with them. Just as your reactions and behaviors are rooted in early childhood relational patterns and coping mechanisms, so too are the reactions and behaviors of your friends, family, romantic partners, and colleagues. They may or may not be aware of the role and impact of their attachment history, but your awareness could lead to improved relationship dynamics and reduced tension and misunderstandings due to unmet and unspoken needs and desires.

Observing Relationship Patterns

One way to identify hidden attachment styles is by observing relationship patterns. People often repeat the dynamics they experienced during childhood. Those with anxious attachment may find themselves in relationships where they feel insecure, while avoidant individuals might end up in partnerships that lack emotional depth. If you notice a friend constantly choosing partners who are unreliable or distant, this could indicate an avoidant attachment. Encourage them to reflect on these patterns, as recognizing them is the first step toward change.

Listening to Communication Styles

Communication is another vital clue when identifying attachment styles. Anxiously attached individuals might frequently express their fears or concerns, seeking validation. Meanwhile, those with avoidant styles may use humor or sarcasm to deflect deeper conversations. They might also downplay the importance of relationships, responding with phrases like "It's no big deal." Understanding these differences can help in addressing the issues that arise in relationships. Foster open dialogues that encourage honest discussions about feelings and needs.

Noticing Emotional Responses

Emotional reactions can also reveal a person's attachment style. Anxiously attached individuals may experience heightened emotions during conflicts, feeling panicked if they perceive a threat to their relationship. On the other hand, avoidant types might withdraw or shut down when faced with intense emotions. It's common for them to respond to stress by becoming disengaged rather than confronting the issue. When you notice these emotional responses, approach the individual with empathy and understanding. Encourage them to express what they feel, helping to create a more supportive interaction.

Observing Open-Ended Questions

How someone responds to open-ended questions can give insight into their attachment style. For example, anxious individuals might struggle with these questions, fearing they won't meet expectations. They may provide overly detailed responses or seem overly concerned about not saying the right thing. Avoidantly attached people might answer but avoid deeper exploration, choosing brevity instead. Staying patient and allowing space for thoughtful responses can help individuals feel more comfortable sharing their inner thoughts.

Paying Attention to Body Language

Body language can be another indicator of attachment styles. Anxiously attached individuals may display nervous gestures, like fidgeting or avoiding eye contact, especially when discussing sensitive topics. Avoidantly attached persons may cross their arms or lean away, indicating a need for space or discomfort. In contrast, people with a secure attachment tend to have open and relaxed body language. Taking note of these cues can guide you in how to approach conversations. Encouraging a relaxed atmosphere can help foster more positive interactions.

CHAPTER 1

Understanding Personal History

A person's background also plays a crucial role in their attachment style. Understanding their past can provide context for their behavior in relationships. For instance, someone who grew up with inconsistent caregiving may struggle with trust. Learning about someone's history can help illuminate their reactions and behaviors in relationships. This knowledge fosters empathy and creates a deeper connection. When discussing the past, listen actively and validate their experiences without judgment.

Encouraging others to reflect on their attachment styles can create new opportunities for growth. You can facilitate discussions around feelings and relationships, offering a safe space for them to explore their thoughts. Asking questions like, "How do you feel when conflicts arise?" or "What do you look for in a partner?" can help guide this process. This form of self-exploration can lead to insightful realizations about their behaviors and patterns, promoting self-awareness.

Supporting friends and partners in understanding their attachment styles can lead to healthier relationships. It might involve sharing resources or suggesting they explore their patterns with a counselor or therapist. Encouraging conversations about attachment styles within friendships can also help create an environment of understanding. General discussions about emotional well-being can normalize these topics, making it easier for everyone to engage in constructive dialogues about their relationships.

Interactive Quiz

Discover Your Attachment Style in Different Contexts

Different social contexts can highlight your attachment style. While it's possible to display different types of attachment in various relationships, it's more likely that how you are in one relationship can affect how you are in other relationships, too. This quiz helps you identify your dominant attachment style, which is evident in more than one social context. For each scenario, choose the option that best describes your typical response. Keep track of your answers to identify your attachment style at the end of the quiz.

Questions:

1. With romantic partners: When your partner needs space, you usually:

   A) Feel anxious and try to reach out frequently.
   B) Respect their space but worry about where the relationship stands.
   C) Feel fine and give them the space they need.
   D) Use the time apart to focus on your own interests.

2. With friends: When a friend cancels plans at the last minute, you:

   A) Feel hurt and wonder if they really care about the friendship.
   B) Get mildly upset but understand things come up.
   C) Don't mind and can easily reschedule without feeling bad.
   D) Feel relieved as you had other things you wanted to do.

CHAPTER 2

3. With family: During family gatherings, you tend to:

   A) Stay close to a few family members and avoid larger groups.
   B) Feel comfortable but sometimes experience conflict.
   C) Mingle easily and engage with everyone.
   D) Stay a bit distant, preferring to observe rather than participate.

4. With colleagues: When working on a team project, you:

   A) Often take charge, fearing others won't pull their weight.
   B) Collaborate but hesitate to voice your ideas.
   C) Freely share your thoughts and enjoy teamwork.
   D) Prefer to work independently and avoid group dynamics.

5. In new relationships: When starting to date someone new, you feel:

   A) Anxious about whether they like you back.
   B) Hopeful but cautious, taking things slowly.
   C) Excited and open to the possibilities.
   D) Indifferent and relaxed about the outcome.

6. In conflicts: When conflicts arise, your instinct is to:

   A) Avoid confrontation at all costs.
   B) Want to resolve things but often feel overwhelmed.
   C) Address the issue head-on and communicate openly.
   D) Give each other space and revisit the topic later.

7. In long-term relationships: In a long-term relationship, you tend to:

   A) Feel a need for constant reassurance of love and commitment.
   B) Sometimes doubt your partner's feelings but usually trust them.
   C) Feel secure and confident about your bond.
   D) Maintain your independence while being supportive of each other.

Scoring: Count how many times you selected each letter (A, B, C, D).

- Mostly As: Anxious attachment style
- Mostly Bs: Ambivalent attachment style
- Mostly Cs: Secure attachment style
- Mostly Ds: Avoidant attachment style

Reflect on your responses to gain insights about your attachment style in different relational dynamics. Use this information to identify potential areas for improvement, such as tendencies that could add more pressure or create misunderstandings in your relationships.

In this chapter, we ventured into the depths of attachment styles, peeling back layers to understand the origins and manifestations of these patterns. While initially defined by terms like anxious, avoidant, and disorganized, each style is a pattern learned from early emotional experiences and environmental influences. The discussion unfolds around how caregiving shapes these attachment behaviors, providing context to why some individuals cling tightly to connections while others shy away.

By acknowledging these differences, the chapter invites readers to reflect on their relational patterns and consider how attachment styles are not rigid constructs but flexible frameworks subject to change and growth. In the following chapter, we will discuss the role and impact of attachment styles in relationships.

02.

The Role of Attachment in Relationships

If I appeal to you for emotional connection and you respond intellectually to a problem, rather than directly to me, on an attachment level I will experience that as "no response." –Sue Johnson

66

The Influence of Attachment on Self-Perception and Internal Dialogue

As you go through life, the way you attach to others greatly shapes how you see yourself and talk to yourself in your mind. Many people think of attachment as something that relates only to childhood and family relationships. However, its effects reach much further than your early years. Understanding how attachment styles impact your self-perception can help you recognize patterns in your life that may be holding you back.

Attachment styles are ways that you relate to others, and they can create patterns that influence your self-identity. This begins in childhood, during your interactions with your primary caregivers. For example, when caregivers are nurturing and responsive, children usually develop a strong sense of self-worth. They learn to see themselves as valuable and capable. This positive reinforcement builds their confidence and shapes a healthy self-image that guides them through life. On the other hand, when caregivers are inconsistent or neglectful, it can lead to feelings of insecurity. These children might grow up with a distorted view of themselves, believing they are not worthy of love or respect (Wu, 2009).

Children who grow up with secure attachment often feel safe in expressing their emotions. They can ask for help or share their thoughts without fear of being judged. This comfort allows them to develop a balanced view of themselves and their abilities. For instance, if they succeed at something, they can celebrate it without dismissing their accomplishment. They internalize positive messages that reinforce their self-worth.

In contrast, those with insecure attachment styles, such as avoidant or ambivalent, typically struggle with negative self-concepts. Avoidant individuals often push away their emotional needs and may present themselves as strong and independent, but deep down, they may feel a lack of emotional connection. This can lead to difficulty in forming close relationships. An example might be a person who achieves great success at work but still feels empty and unfulfilled because they shut themselves off emotionally. They often disregard their feelings, thinking that vulnerability is a weakness.

Ambivalent individuals, on the other hand, may find themselves caught in a cycle of anxiety and uncertainty. They often oscillate between high and low self-esteem. This inconsistency can result in emotional distress. For example, someone with an ambivalent attachment might feel excellent after receiving praise yet immediately doubt their abilities the next day. Such insecurity can lead to a troubled internal dialogue filled with worry and self-criticism.

These attachment-related patterns can cultivate self-doubt. When you question your self-worth, it significantly impacts your personal growth and relationships. You may avoid taking risks or trying new things, fearing failure or rejection. For instance, someone with a negative self-image might hesitate to apply for a promotion at work or hesitate to make new friends, thinking they aren't good enough or that they won't be liked.

The effects of these attachment styles extend beyond just personal feelings; they can influence how you relate to others. People with secure attachments often have healthier relationships. They communicate clearly and tend to resolve conflicts effectively. In contrast, those with insecure attachments may struggle with jealousy or excessive dependence on others for validation. They might find themselves in relationships that reinforce their negative self-perception rather than uplift it.

CHAPTER 2

Internal Dialogue Dynamics

Internal dialogues further reveal the influence of these attachment styles on self-identity. Anxious individuals often indulge in negative self-talk filled with doubt and fear, questioning their adequacy and seeking reassurance. This cycle of self-doubt can become habitual, reinforcing insecurities and limiting potential. Avoidant individuals, on the other hand, may suppress their emotions, avoiding introspection altogether. Their internal dialogue might seem calm on the surface but is marked by denial and emotional detachment.

However, acknowledging these tendencies provides an opportunity for change. There lies a potential to transition from critical internal dialogues to constructive ones through deliberate practice and awareness. By actively recognizing and challenging harmful narratives, individuals can gradually shift toward more positive self-perception. Reframing internal narratives requires intentional effort but promises substantial benefits in reshaping one's self-image.

Moreover, understanding your attachment style facilitates greater self-awareness. Recognizing the connection between your early attachment experiences and current self-identity encourages you to explore your internal dialogues objectively. It offers insight into how past relationships continue to influence your present thoughts and behaviors. With this awareness comes the power to initiate positive shifts, proactively rewriting detrimental scripts perpetuated since childhood.

Deliberate reframing involves replacing negative self-statements with affirming and empowering ones. For example, someone prone to anxious attachment might replace, "I am not good enough," with, "I am learning and growing every day." Over time, such practice alters the neural pathways associated with self-perception, promoting healthier self-esteem and enriching life experiences.

Engaging in mindfulness techniques enhances emotional regulation, allowing you to manage heightened stress responses typical of insecure attachments (Jethava et al., 2022). Techniques like journaling provide a reflective space where you can reassess and reframe your thoughts. Seeking support from professionals, such as therapists trained in attachment-focused therapy, can augment this journey by providing tailored strategies to overcome deeply ingrained patterns.

Additionally, cultivating empathy toward yourself is essential. Insecure attachment often breeds harsh self-criticism, undermining personal worth. Adopting a compassionate approach, akin to how securely attached individuals perceive themselves, nurtures a supportive internal environment. It is crucial to remember that changing internal dialogues and enhancing self-identity is a gradual process, demanding patience and perseverance.

Ultimately, the journey toward reshaping self-identity through awareness and reframing of internal narratives aligns with the broader goal of fostering personal growth and emotional healing. As you embark on this transformative path, you gain the ability to make informed choices in relationships, breaking free from repetitive cycles rooted in insecure attachments. Embracing such changes not only enriches your self-concept but also extends its positive effects across social and professional domains.

Manifestations of Attachment in the Workplace

In the workplace, attachment styles play a significant role in determining how individuals interact with their colleagues and respond to group dynamics. Anxious attachment, for example, often manifests as a strong need for approval and validation from others. Such individuals might constantly seek reassurance from teammates or managers, which can disrupt team harmony and create tension among coworkers.

This persistent need for affirmation can lead to a climate of anxiety, affecting the group's overall productivity and morale. On the other hand, avoidant individuals tend to withdraw from social interactions and collaboration efforts. They may appear detached or uninterested in group goals, preferring to work independently. Their reluctance to fully engage can hinder effective teamwork and stall communication efforts, as their hesitation can be perceived as a lack of interest or commitment to shared objectives.

Communication is another key area where attachment styles significantly impact workplace interactions. People with anxious attachments may communicate in ways that seem overly needy or uncertain, frequently asking for feedback or validation. Conversely, avoidant individuals often adopt a distant or dismissive communication style, avoiding deep discussions or sharing personal opinions.

These varied approaches can lead to misunderstandings and misinterpretations within teams, emphasizing the necessity of cultivating clear and open communication channels. Effective communication strategies can help bridge these differences by establishing a common understanding and reducing potential conflicts arising from miscommunication.

Moreover, practicing empathy in the workplace is essential for building open dialogues and meaningful connections among employees with diverse attachment styles. Empathy allows team members to appreciate each other's unique emotional responses and perspectives, promoting a more inclusive and supportive environment. For instance, empathetic leaders who recognize the anxiety-driven needs of some employees can respond with patience and provide the necessary support, helping them feel valued and secure. Similarly, understanding the independence sought by avoidant individuals can guide managers to offer space and autonomy, respecting their preference for self-reliance while encouraging constructive participation.

Secure attachment styles naturally enhance collaboration and productivity within professional settings. Individuals with secure attachments generally exhibit confidence, reliability, and a willingness to engage openly with peers. They are comfortable handling feedback and can navigate conflicts constructively, acting as stabilizing forces within their teams. Securely attached employees often serve as role models, demonstrating effective communication and adaptability, which fosters a positive and cohesive work culture. Their presence helps bridge gaps between less secure colleagues, facilitating smoother interactions and enhancing overall team performance.

Practically applying this understanding of attachment styles involves creating an environment that values trust, transparency, and mutual respect. Managers and leaders can implement training programs to raise awareness about attachment theories and their implications in professional contexts. By learning to identify and accommodate different attachment-related behaviors, teams can develop tailored strategies that leverage strengths and address challenges. Regular check-ins, feedback sessions, and team-building activities can also nurture a sense of belonging and safety, allowing employees to express themselves authentically without fear of judgment or rejection.

Conceptualizing "Attachment Burnout"

In today's world, attachment burnout has become a rising concern. It can be described as the emotional fatigue that surfaces when unresolved attachment issues are faced with continual stress (Ho, 2024). This phenomenon can be particularly visible in high-pressure environments, where persistent demands and complex relationships magnify these underlying insecurities.

Attachment burnout is similar to occupational burnout but specifically targets the emotional ties and expectations we carry in relationships. Imagine being on a treadmill you can't seem to step off from—feeling emotionally drained and stuck. In professional settings, this can lead to a noticeable drop in efficiency, impacting teamwork and individual productivity.

Recognizing signs of burnout within team dynamics is critical. These signs often include irritability, reduced enthusiasm, and, at times, withdrawal from group activities. Such behaviors can undermine team morale and productivity, making it essential for managers and team members to spot these early indicators. Understanding these symptoms isn't just about empathy; it's about maintaining harmony and well-being, which are vital for achieving collective goals.

A proactive approach toward self-awareness is fundamental to managing and preventing attachment burnout. Mindfulness practices serve as a valuable tool here. By fostering an ability to live in the present moment without judgment, mindfulness allows individuals to break cycles of anxiety and stress. For instance, simple exercises such as deep breathing can significantly decrease stress levels. Studies have shown that incorporating mindfulness techniques into daily routines enhances emotional regulation and resilience, setting a solid foundation for dealing with relationship-induced stressors (Channawar, 2023).

Burnout can affect anyone, but for Anna, a marketing executive, it was particularly challenging. Her professional life was demanding, requiring her to meet tight deadlines and juggle various projects. However, the pressure at work was not the only issue she faced. Anna had unresolved childhood attachment issues that significantly contributed to her struggles. These attachment issues stemmed from her early relationships, making it hard for her to manage stress and create healthy boundaries in her work environment.

In her case, being overly committed and feeling the need to please others were traits she developed as a child. This pattern followed her into adulthood and intensified under the pressures of her job. For many people, the demands of their careers can bring to the surface unresolved emotional issues. Anna realized that her feelings of exhaustion and anxiety at work were not just about her workload but were tied to deeper emotional roots.

Discovering therapy was a turning point for Anna. She began attending sessions focused on her attachment style, which is how people form emotional bonds and relationships. With the help of her therapist, Anna learned to identify her patterns and how they were affecting her life. Therapy allowed her to explore her past and understand how her childhood experiences shaped her perceptions and actions today.

For Anna, it was essential to confront her feelings in a safe space. During her sessions, she worked on recognizing her attachment styles—anxious, avoidant, or secure—and how these impacted her relationships at work and with friends. By understanding these dynamics, she could start to make changes.

Navigating Friendships Through an Attachment Lens

Understanding how attachment styles influence friendships provides illuminating insights into the dynamics we experience with close companions. At the heart of these interactions lies our early attachments, which play a pivotal role in shaping who we choose as friends and how we maintain these bonds.

For those with an anxious attachment style, friendships often become a delicate balance of seeking reassurance and avoiding perceived abandonment. Anxious individuals may depend heavily on their friends for validation, stemming from a deep-seated fear of being left alone. This can sometimes lead to behaviors where they might overly cling to friendships or compensate by prioritizing others' needs over their own. While this devotion can be endearing, it risks becoming overwhelming for their peers, potentially driving them away and inadvertently confirming the anxious person's fears. The cycle perpetuates: Overdependence leads to withdrawal by friends, fostering more anxiety about abandonment.

On the other side of the spectrum, avoidantly attached individuals face their unique set of challenges. Often valuing independence, they may find it challenging to embrace the emotional depths that friendships require. Their struggle isn't due to a lack of care or interest, but rather a discomfort with vulnerability and intimacy. They might keep friends at arm's length, fearing that opening up would compromise their autonomy.

Consequently, while they might enjoy social gatherings, true connection remains elusive. Friends may perceive them as distant or uninterested, even if that's far from the truth. These perceptions could hinder the formation of long-lasting emotional connections, placing avoidant individuals in a bind between their desire for closeness and their instinctual retreat.

Resolving Friendship Conflicts

Conflict is an inevitable aspect of any friendship, yet attachment styles dictate how these conflicts are managed. Anxiously attached individuals might view disagreements as catastrophic, spiraling into panic at the thought of losing the relationship. Their responses can range from appeasement—agreeing just to preserve peace—to defensive tactics like excessive explanations or apologies.

Avoidant friends, conversely, might withdraw when tensions arise, avoiding confrontation entirely. For them, conflict can feel intrusive, prompting them to seek space rather than address distressing emotions. Recognizing these patterns is essential, not only for personal growth but also for the health of the friendship. Tailoring resolution strategies to accommodate these tendencies can foster understanding and facilitate healing, ensuring that disagreements don't mark the end, but rather a chance to strengthen bonds.

The profound role of vulnerability cannot be understated in enhancing friendships across all attachment styles. When friends take the courageous step to share their innermost feelings and experiences, they open pathways to deeper understanding and trust. For anxiously attached individuals, practicing vulnerability means recognizing when to express concerns without overwhelming their friends.

By voicing their insecurities and fears in measured ways, they invite empathy from their peers, transforming potential friction into nurturing support. Avoidant individuals face a different challenge: allowing themselves to lean on others despite their self-sufficient facade. By gradually sharing personal stories or admitting struggles, they can bridge the emotional gap and present themselves as more relatable and approachable.

Creating friendships that thrive amidst the complexities of attachment requires conscious effort and a willingness to adapt. For everyone involved, self-awareness becomes crucial; understanding your attachment style allows for better navigation through the intricate dance of friendship. It's through this view that you can recognize your behavioral patterns and recalibrate your responses to better suit your relationships.

Encouraging open dialogues about these styles with your friends—while daunting—can demystify intentions behind your actions or theirs and alleviate misinterpretations. By creating spaces where such conversations are welcomed, you effectively lay down the foundation for more resilient and emotionally connected friendships.

Moreover, it's important to note that no attachment style is inherently superior or inferior. Each presents its unique strengths and challenges. Securely attached individuals, typically capable of managing emotions well, can serve as anchors within their social circles. However, those with insecure styles shouldn't feel discouraged. Growth is possible, and friendships provide fertile ground for development.

Through conscious reflection and genuine attempts to understand yourself and others, you can transform perceived attachment limitations into opportunities for evolution. Witnessing friends' empathetic responses during vulnerable moments can reaffirm your belief in the depth and resilience of these bonds.

Attachment Styles and Romantic Attraction

Attachment styles play a significant role in how people feel attracted to each other. A secure individual often attracts partners who have anxious or avoidant attachment styles. This happens because secure people create a sense of safety that anxious people crave. For anxious individuals, having a secure partner feels comforting and reassuring. Avoidant partners also appreciate the presence of a secure person.

They may feel less threatened and more at ease in the relationship. However, the dynamics between anxious and avoidant individuals can be complicated. Anxiously attached individuals might find themselves drawn to the mysterious and exciting nature of avoidant partners. Initially, this can feel exhilarating. But, as the relationship progresses, the attraction can lead to confusion.

The relationship between an anxious person and an avoidant partner often involves a push-and-pull dynamic. An anxious partner may experience overwhelming longing for closeness, while the avoidant partner may withdraw to maintain their independence. This back-and-forth can be thrilling at first, but it often leads to frustration. The anxious partner may feel a deep connection that becomes increasingly unsatisfying.

The differences stemming from their attachment styles are likely to surface over time. By understanding these patterns, individuals can navigate their feelings more effectively. Learning about these attachment styles can help people in romantic relationships recognize potential pitfalls and communicate better, paving the way for healthier connections.

CHAPTER 2

Being aware of your own attachment style is crucial for improving romantic relationships. Each person's early experiences shape how they interact with others, particularly in love. Identifying your attachment style can be a first step toward meaningful change. For instance, if you identify as having an anxious attachment style, you might notice that you often seek constant reassurance from your partner. Recognizing this behavior is important. Instead of always looking for affirmation, you can work on expressing your needs more clearly. Being self-aware allows you to address issues and avoid unhealthy patterns.

Sometimes, people may find it hard to manage their attachment styles on their own. In such cases, seeking professional help can be beneficial. A therapist can offer guidance in understanding your attachment patterns and provide strategies for positive change. Therapy can lead to greater emotional stability and healthier relationships overall.

Couples therapy might also be an option for partners who want to understand each other better. The process of discussing and exploring each person's attachment style can open up pathways for improved communication. Couples who understand each other's attachment styles can create a nurturing and stable environment together.

Practical Steps for Building Better Relationships

To build and maintain healthier romantic relationships, there are practical steps based on the understanding of attachment styles that anyone can take. Below are four key steps to focus on.

Establish Open Communication

To build and maintain healthier romantic relationships, one of the first things to focus on is open communication. Good communication is essential as it sets the foundation for understanding each other. One practical step is to establish a routine where both partners feel comfortable discussing their feelings and concerns. This could be done by setting aside some time each week for a check-in.

During these sessions, you can express your thoughts freely. For example, you might set up a specific time on Sunday afternoons when both of you can sit down and talk about what's on your mind. This way, each partner has the opportunity to articulate their needs and desires within a safe and supportive environment.

Demonstrate Patience and Empathy

In addition to open communication, practicing patience and empathy is vital in a relationship. It can be beneficial to recognize that your partner's behavior is often influenced by their attachment style. For instance, if your partner seems distant or unresponsive, it may be more about their own feelings of discomfort rather than a lack of interest in you. They might have an avoidant attachment style, which can make them appear detached.

It's crucial not to take these moments personally. Instead, try to adopt an empathetic approach. This means putting yourself in their shoes and understanding that their behavior isn't necessarily a reflection of their love for you. By approaching such situations with kindness, you can foster a more loving dynamic. This could involve reassuring your partner that it's okay to express their feelings, which can help create an environment where both feel understood and valued.

Encourage Mutual Growth

Each person in the relationship should make an effort to understand their own attachment style, as well as their partner's. Knowing your attachment style can provide insights into your reactions in various situations. For example, if you recognize that you have an anxious attachment style, you may understand why you often seek reassurance. Similarly, learning about your partner's style can enhance your empathy. You could spend time together reading helpful resources or discussing what you've learned about each other. This dedication to self-improvement not only increases self-awareness but also deepens the emotional connection between partners.

Establish Shared Goals

Setting relationship goals gives both of you something to work toward together. These goals could range from agreeing on personal and relationship boundaries to discussing future plans or working on individual development. For example, perhaps you both decide to prioritize time together each week by planning a date night or setting health goals for exercise. Having shared objectives allows you both to focus on what you want to achieve as a team. It encourages teamwork and helps you gain a better understanding of each other's needs and desires.

Taking the time to define these goals can also provide clarity in your relationship. From the beginning, you might want to sit down and write out what both of you envision for your future. Questions like, "Where do we want to be in five years?" or, "What activities can we do together to strengthen our bond?" can open the floor for discussion. Writing down these goals can help you remember them and assess your progress over time. It can also encourage accountability. By knowing what you both want to work toward, you can support each other in your individual journeys while simultaneously fostering your shared connection.

Make Gratitude a Daily Practice

Practicing gratitude is a practical and often overlooked step in nurturing healthy relationships. It's easy to take each other for granted, especially when life gets busy. Making a habit of regularly expressing gratitude for your partner can reinforce goodwill and affection. You might decide to share one thing you appreciate about each other at the end of your weekly check-ins. This simple act of acknowledgment not only builds positive feelings but also encourages a deeper appreciation for one another. For instance, thanking your partner for their support during a difficult week can strengthen your emotional bond.

Schedule Quality Time

Additionally, spending quality time together is crucial for the health of your relationship. This doesn't always mean going out; it can simply be making time to enjoy each other's company at home. You might cook a meal together, watch a movie, or even take a walk. These moments of connection can become cherished traditions. For example, you might implement a routine where you spend Friday nights together cooking and trying new recipes. These rituals build shared experiences that instill a sense of togetherness and belonging, which can be incredibly grounding in a romantic relationship.

Prioritize Conflict Resolution

Conflicts are a natural part of any relationship, but how you handle them makes a significant difference. When disagreements arise, try to approach them calmly and respectfully. Use "I" statements to express how you feel without blaming your partner. For example, saying, "I feel upset when we don't communicate about our plans," can open up a dialogue without sounding accusatory. Aim to find a compromise that works for both of you. This might require some patience and active listening. By valuing each other's perspectives, you can transform conflicts into opportunities for growth and understanding.

Interactive Exercise

Self-Compassion Journaling Prompts

Journaling can be a powerful tool for self-reflection and healing, particularly when it comes to understanding our personal interactions and attachment styles. By engaging in this guided journaling exercise, you will have the opportunity to explore your thoughts and feelings with compassion. These self-compassion journaling prompts will help you uncover patterns in your relationships, recognize your emotional needs, and cultivate a kinder inner dialogue. Take your time with each prompt, allowing yourself to reflect deeply and write freely.

Prompts:

1. Describe a recent interaction with someone that triggered a strong emotion in you. What feelings did you experience, and what thoughts were running through your mind during this interaction?

2. Think about a situation where you felt misunderstood or rejected. Write a compassionate letter to yourself as if you were comforting a friend in the same situation. What would you say to ease their pain and promote self-acceptance?

3. List five emotional needs that are important to you in relationships (e.g., trust, communication, or affection). Reflect on whether these needs are being met in your current relationships or if there are barriers preventing this.

4. Imagine what a secure attachment would look like in your life. What qualities or characteristics do you envision in your relationships? Describe how you would feel and how your interactions would change.

5.   Identify a recurring negative thought you have about yourself, especially in relation to your connections with others. Challenge this thought by writing a reframed, positive affirmation that counters it.

6.   Write a list of three people in your life who contribute positively to your emotional well-being. Reflect on specific qualities they possess or actions they have taken that make you feel appreciated and valued.

7.   Consider a relationship where you need to set a boundary. Describe how you can communicate this need compassionately without feeling guilty or selfish. What steps will you take to implement this boundary respectfully?

8.   Think of a situation where you felt wronged by someone. Explore your feelings and what it would mean to forgive them. Write about the potential healing that could come from releasing this burden.

9.   Finally, set intentions for how you want to approach your relationships moving forward. What actions or mindset shifts will you adopt to foster healthier connections and a sense of security in your interactions with others?

_____

_____

_____

_____

_____

_____

_____

SELF-COMPASSION JOURNALING PROMPTS

SELF-COMPASSION JOURNALING PROMPTS

_____

_____

_____

_____

_____

_____

_____

In this enlightening chapter, we examined how different attachment styles subtly shape our self-talk, self-image, and relationship dynamics. Exploring these varied attachment types uncovers their hidden influences on internal dialogue, providing insights into how they might skew our self-perceptions. Additionally, this discussion extends to broader domains such as workplace dynamics, friendships, and romantic relationships, shedding light on the manifestation of attachment behaviors in different social settings.

By understanding these perspectives, you will learn to identify the patterns that may be affecting your personal growth and relationships. Moreover, practical strategies for transforming critical self-dialogues into constructive conversations are introduced, fostering positive shifts in one's self-identity and interpersonal ties. Through this examination, you gain the tools to initiate and embrace meaningful changes, enhancing not only your sense of self but also your external connections. In the next chapter, we will take a closer look at the influence of early childhood experiences on adult relationships.

03.

Emotional Archaeology—Excavating the Impact of Early Experiences

If you do not learn to meet your needs directly, you will learn to meet them neurotically. You will develop routines and relationships and rituals that are designed to help you get just enough of what you want without having to ask for it directly. –Heidi Priebe

"

Mapping the Influence of Childhood Experiences on Adult Attachments

Our childhoods, filled with interactions and emotions, shape much more than our memories; they form the roots of how we connect with others as adults. Imagine these formative years as laying down the first bricks of a building—invisible yet crucial to its stability. They influence not just the facade but the entire structural integrity of our future relationships. For some, this foundation is sound, creating safe havens of warmth and trust. For others, cracks might appear, leading to relational patterns that seem broken or unreliable. Understanding these influences allows us to take a closer look at what lies beneath the surface, sparking curiosity about our attachment styles.

From birth, humans rely on caregivers not just for basic needs but also for emotional nurturing. The quality of these interactions lays the groundwork for future relational behavior. A caregiver's responsiveness helps a child develop a positive self-image and trust in others. For instance, securely attached children learn that they can depend on their caregivers for comfort and protection. As adults, they often enter relationships with confidence, seeking connections built on mutual respect and intimacy (Cleveland Clinic, 2022).

Conversely, less attentive caregiving can create uncertainty and mistrust. Anxiously attached individuals often seek constant reassurance and show a heightened sensitivity to rejection due to past inconsistencies in caregiving. Avoidantly attached people might shun closeness, having learned to rely primarily on themselves when their needs were unmet during childhood. Disorganized attachment is often marked by erratic behaviors in caregiving, leaving children without a reliable strategy for managing stress. This confusion can translate into chaotic relationships in adulthood (Doyle & Cicchetti, 2017).

Understanding specific caregiving behaviors can illuminate why some individuals experience secure attachment while others do not. When caregivers respond sensitively and appropriately to a child's needs, they foster an environment of safety and predictability. For example, a parent who promptly attends to a crying infant teaches them that their feelings matter and will be acknowledged. Conversely, failure to consistently respond to a child's emotional needs may lead to attachment insecurity. If a child learns that comfort is unreliable, this expectation can transfer to adult relationships, causing either clinging behaviors out of fear of abandonment or withdrawal to protect oneself from anticipated neglect.

A significant step toward building healthier relationships lies in personal reflection. By examining your childhood interactions, you can better understand your current relationship patterns. Reflecting on questions like, "How did my caregivers respond to my emotional needs?" or, "What behaviors did I learn about giving and receiving love?" can offer clarity on ingrained habits and beliefs. This introspection allows you to recognize which aspects of your attachment style serve you well and which might hinder your ability to form fulfilling connections.

Addressing Generational Trauma and Its Role in Creating Attachment Issues

The shadows of family history and ancestral experiences can profoundly shape how you relate to others today. Inherited emotional patterns, often passed down from generation to generation, can subtly influence these attachments, sometimes tipping the balance toward insecurity and distrust without your conscious awareness (Copley, 2024).

Understanding these inherited patterns can be compared to uncovering layers of unseen influences that direct your behaviors and relationships. For instance, if a grandparent experienced significant trauma or emotional upheaval, the reverberations of that experience could unknowingly impact you and subsequent generations. This generational echo can manifest as anxiety, hesitance in forming close bonds, or an overarching sense of mistrust. Recognizing these patterns isn't about assigning blame or guilt; rather, it's about acknowledging their presence in your current relationships so that you can address them and cultivate healthier interactions.

A key element in this exploration is the concept of intergenerational trauma—how unresolved traumas continue to ripple through families, affecting those who may never have directly experienced the original events. Take, for example, descendants of communities affected by major historical traumas like slavery, genocide, or war. They may exhibit behaviors or emotional responses rooted in survival mechanisms from those times. While not directly exposed to these situations themselves, they might carry behavioral legacies passed down as coping strategies (Yehuda & Lehrner, 2018).

Breaking free from these cycles requires intentional action and heartfelt reflection. It involves understanding the persistence of these traumas and consciously choosing to not let them dictate present and future relationship dynamics. You are encouraged to engage in open dialogues about past experiences, creating spaces where stories can be shared and reinterpreted. By doing so, you create environments where healing can emerge from honest understanding and empathy.

CHAPTER 3

Cultural context also plays a pivotal role in shaping your attachment styles and emotional responses. Every culture has its own set of norms and expectations around relationships, emotional expression, and family roles. These cultural narratives can reinforce attachment issues if they're rooted in outdated or harmful practices. For example, cultures that prioritize stoicism and discourage the display of vulnerability might leave individuals struggling with emotional intimacy and connection, which can promote avoidant relational coping behaviors.

Recognizing this means observing not only your personal family histories but also the broader cultural factors at play. Understanding how these larger societal forces shape your behaviors allows for a more comprehensive approach to tackling attachment issues. It invites you to question the narratives you've been taught and encourages you to forge new paths that align with healthier emotional expressions and connections.

Healing Generational Wounds by Connecting with Your Roots

Generational wounds often come from the struggles, traumas, and experiences passed down through family lines. Understanding and connecting with your roots can help you address and heal these wounds, leading to a more fulfilling life. Connecting with your roots involves exploring your ancestry, understanding family histories, and learning about cultural traditions. It's about finding a sense of belonging and identity that has sometimes been lost or overshadowed by past pain.

When you start this journey, the first step is to gather information about your family history. This can involve talking to family members, especially older generations who might have stories to share. These conversations are important because they can reveal the patterns of behavior and challenges that have shaped your family over the years. For instance, if you find out that many family members struggled with certain issues, such as addiction or mental health challenges, this knowledge can help you understand your own experiences better. Maybe you tend to turn to substances to cope with relationship stress or frequently experience anxiety. Take notes during these discussions and consider asking open-ended questions to encourage sharing.

Learning about the struggles that previous generations faced can also provide context for your own life. Write down the relationship challenges that your ancestors endured and reflect on how those events may have influenced your family's dynamics. When you recognize these connections, it becomes easier to identify patterns in your own life. For instance, if you notice a cycle of fear or avoidance when faced with difficult situations, understanding that this behavior might stem from past traumas can be enlightening. This awareness can lead to personal growth, as you actively work to change these inherited patterns.

When you deepen your understanding of your history, consider building connections with your extended family, as this can also be a significant part of your healing process. Attend family reunions or gatherings to strengthen bonds with your relatives so you can receive support or possibly start practicing new bonding behaviors, which is vital in healing generational wounds. If possible, create opportunities for family storytelling, where each member can share their experiences and memories. This sharing can strengthen connections and highlight the resilience of your family. Sharing these stories can also be empowering; it helps to realize that you are part of a larger narrative and that your experiences matter.

Connecting with your roots may also lead to seeking out support groups or therapy. Sometimes, the healing journey can bring up difficult emotions that are hard to process alone. Speaking with a licensed therapist who specializes in family dynamics can provide valuable insights. They can guide you through understanding how your family's history impacts you and help identify coping strategies for moving forward. Group settings can also offer support from others who are sharing similar experiences. These settings can foster a sense of community and validation.

Practicing self-compassion is an essential component of healing generational wounds. It's important to remember that you are not responsible for the pain of those who came before you. Acknowledge that healing is a process and be kind to yourself as you navigate your feelings. Allow yourself to celebrate progress, no matter how small it may seem. You might find it helpful to create affirmations that remind you of your worth and resilience. Using positive affirmations during difficult times can shift your mindset and empower you by reinforcing your strength and potential.

Techniques to Reshape Childhood Narratives for Healing

In your journey to reshape identity and attachment outcomes rooted in childhood narratives, cognitive restructuring stands out as a valuable tool. This method involves actively challenging and reframing the negative beliefs or stories you cling to from your past. Often, these childhood narratives are self-imposed limitations that manifest into adulthood, dictating how you form relationships and perceive yourself. By recognizing these distorted beliefs—and understanding that they're not an intrinsic part of who you are—cognitive restructuring allows for the development of new, healthier perspectives (Villines, 2022).

Visualization

Visualization is a form of cognitive restructuring that allows you to reimagine past situations where you felt vulnerable with scenarios that evoke security and empowerment instead. Imagine walking through a past event with the knowledge and strength you possess today; it transforms the narrative from one of helplessness to one of control and resilience (Georgieva & Georgiev, 2019). Through repetitive practice, these visualizations imprint a sense of peace related to past experiences, essentially rewriting the emotional script tied to those memories, which can lead to significant changes in how you perceive your present and future selves.

Record and listen to the following visualization script to help you shift your narrative about relationships and attachment:

> Find a comfortable position where you can relax without distractions. Close your eyes and take a deep breath in, feeling your lungs expand. Hold it for a moment, then exhale slowly, letting go of any tension.

Now, bring to mind a past event from your childhood where you felt vulnerable in a relationship. Allow yourself to visualize the details of that moment—the sights, sounds, and emotions associated with it. Acknowledge how it made you feel, but know that you are safe now.

Imagine a warm, protective light surrounding you. This light represents your strength and knowledge gained over the years. As you focus on this light, feel it infusing you with confidence and security.

Now, see yourself in that past event, but this time, visualize the situation playing out differently. Picture yourself standing tall, expressing your needs and boundaries with ease. Imagine the people involved responding positively, creating a supportive and understanding atmosphere.

As you continue to visualize this new narrative, feel the weight of past helplessness lifting. With each breath, embrace a sense of empowerment and resilience. Know that you have the ability to rewrite your story.

When you are ready, slowly bring your awareness back to the present moment. Take a deep breath in again and exhale, feeling grounded and calm. Open your eyes, carrying with you the strength and security from this visualization.

Storytelling for Healing

Effective storytelling serves not only as a therapeutic outlet but also as a powerful transformation vehicle. By sharing personal narratives—whether verbally or through writing—you can externalize your lived experiences, viewing them from a distance rather than internalizing them as defining elements of your identity. This process not only lightens your emotional load but also enhances clarity about your personal story. Engaging in storytelling within supportive spaces or communities can promote healing, emphasizing that you are not alone in your feelings or experiences (Georgieva & Georgiev, 2019). Furthermore, when narratives are shared with close friends and family, they can be reshaped collaboratively, offering fresh insights and potential paths toward resolution and growth.

Concurrently, positive self-talk complements narrative reconstruction by directly influencing your day-to-day mindset and self-perception. The power of language in molding your identity should not be underestimated. Regularly practicing affirmations or engaging in constructive self-dialogue can fortify self-worth and bolster confidence. Language can shape reality; thus, choosing words that uplift and empower you encourages a shift in how you perceive your abilities and potential. Consciously nurturing a narrative filled with self-compassion and validation gradually alters your internal dialogues, redirecting you away from criticism and toward acceptance and encouragement.

Here are 10 affirmations that you can repeat to yourself every morning to change your language and beliefs about relationships:

1. *I deserve love and respect in all my relationships.*
2. *I attract healthy and fulfilling connections effortlessly.*
3. *I communicate openly and honestly, fostering deeper understanding.*
4. *I release all fears and insecurities, embracing trust and vulnerability.*
5. *My worth is inherent, and I choose to be surrounded by positivity.*
6. *I cultivate relationships that inspire and uplift me.*
7. *I create boundaries that protect my energy and well-being.*
8. *I am open to giving and receiving love in its many forms.*
9. *I learn and grow from every relationship experience.*
10. *I am grateful for the love in my life and the connections I nurture.*

To illustrate this transformative process, consider an individual who grew up in an environment where mistakes were severely criticized. Throughout their life, they carry an internal narrative that they are inherently flawed. Visualization could help them revisit a critical event, but this time seeing themselves respond with assurance and calm. Through storytelling, they could share this journey with others who relate, realizing the universality of such struggles. Positive self-talk might mean replacing "I'm a failure" with "I am learning and evolving." This multifaceted approach does not promise instant results; rather, it's a gradual, ongoing commitment to personal change. Identifying the roots of dysfunctional narratives is an initial step, but persistence in practicing new skills ensures lasting impact.

Reparenting Yourself as a Tool for Secure Attachments

As you build connections with others, you equally need to nurture a relationship with yourself—though this can be challenging for some. A lack of consistent emotional connection, acknowledgment, affection, or support during childhood often leads you to search for these essentials in the world around you, leaning on others to satisfy your unfulfilled desires. However, no amount of external validation can truly suffice. Relying on others for your self-worth and happiness places your emotional well-being in someone else's hands, which can cause codependency and unhealthy attachment. Fortunately, you can regain this lost agency by offering yourself the love, attention, and attachment you missed out on as a child.

Understanding how to nurture and reparent your inner child is fundamental in forming secure attachment styles as adults. Reparenting focuses on healing wounds from your past, allowing you to create healthier relationships with yourself and others. The concept, particularly in an emotional context, plays a pivotal role in this process. It involves giving yourself the love, care, and validation you may have missed during childhood, signifying self-acceptance, and helping you develop a nurturing and compassionate relationship with yourself.

Self-compassion is key in reparenting. When you treat yourself with the same kindness and understanding you would offer a beloved friend or family member, you cultivate a deeper sense of self-worth. True self-compassion involves forgiving yourself for past mistakes and acknowledging that everyone has moments of struggle. Engaging in activities that promote self-compassion like writing affirmations, practicing gratitude, or surrounding yourself with positive influences can go a long way in developing a compassionate mindset.

CHAPTER 3

Developing a caring inner voice is essential in meeting your emotional needs. Often, we tend to be our harshest critics, which can hinder personal growth. Cultivating a nurturing inner dialogue involves replacing negative self-talk with supportive and encouraging messages. Whenever you catch yourself being overly critical, try to reframe those thoughts with compassion and understanding. This shift in perspective strengthens your mental resilience and boosts self-esteem, laying the foundation for secure attachments.

Meeting your emotional needs requires identifying what truly makes you feel valued and fulfilled. This can vary greatly from person to person, so it's vital to take the time to understand your unique desires and goals. Whether it's spending quality time with loved ones, pursuing hobbies, or simply enjoying solitude, ensure that you prioritize these needs regularly. Creating a balance between giving and receiving support helps reinforce your sense of security and self-worth.

Reparenting isn't an overnight solution; it takes a real and intense love for yourself, which needs to be built over time through a commitment to the continuous journey of self-discovery and healing. Before you can sincerely love and appreciate who you are, you need to work through the many years of denying, judging, blaming, shaming, or abandoning yourself. These maladaptive behaviors cause a split identity where you disconnect from yourself, and it takes time to recover your split selves. Fortunately, techniques like cognitive restructuring or cognitive behavioral therapy that effectively reprogram your subconscious can help you restore a sense of wholeness and cultivate self-love.

As you become more attuned to your inner world, you're likely to develop heightened empathy and understanding toward others. In turn, this inspires deeper and more meaningful interactions. Moreover, this journey emphasizes the importance of setting boundaries, both with yourself and others. Healthy boundaries protect your emotional space, ensuring that you don't overextend yourself. They allow you to communicate your needs effectively while respecting those of others, creating an environment of mutual respect and cooperation.

Interactive Exercise

Family Attachment Map for Generational Insights

This exercise guides you in constructing a family attachment map to identify and record the attachment styles of your family members and take note of bonds that are strong and weak to understand your generational family dynamics better. Read through the instructions and follow the steps outlined.

Instructions:

1. Gather materials such as large paper (or poster board), markers, colored pens, sticky notes, and a ruler for creating neat lines.

2. Generate a list of immediate family members (parents, siblings, and children), then extend this to include significant relationships (grandparents, aunts, uncles, and close family friends).

3. Next to each family member's name, write down their predominant attachment style, according to what you have observed over the years. Use different colors or symbols to represent each attachment style.

4. Create your family attachment map by drawing a central circle for yourself and then branch out to include family members, connecting with lines. Make sure that you use different colors or symbols to indicate the attachment styles of each family member.

5. Observe connections (strong lines) versus disconnections (dotted lines). Make a note of any associations between attachment styles (e.g., two avoidant styles connected).

FAMILY ATTACHMENT MAP FOR GENERATIONAL INSIGHTS

6. Consider how the attachment styles of parents may have influenced your own style. Add layers by indicating which parental styles contributed to your feelings of attachment. Reflect on how these patterns impact current relationships.

Write down any insights about recurring themes, such as avoidance or anxiety in communication. Additionally, you can consider ways to address disconnections or strengthen connections, by, for example, setting goals for improving relationships where needed based on your findings. Feel free to use your family attachment map as a dynamic tool to better understand the patterns in your family relationships. Revisit and update your map as relationships evolve and you gain new insights.

_____

_____

_____

_____

_____

_____

_____

_____

_____

_____

FAMILY ATTACHMENT MAP FOR GENERATIONAL INSIGHTS

This chapter has taken you on a journey through childhood experiences and how they shape your adult relationships. By looking closely at how you were cared for as children, you have gained insights into why you might react the way you do in your current relationships. From understanding attachment styles like secure, anxious, avoidant, or disorganized, you are now more equipped to see patterns that might be limiting you. Recognizing these traits is the first step in changing them, allowing you to create a path toward healthier, more fulfilling connections.

As you reflect on your past, it's essential to approach it not with blame but with curiosity and compassion. The experiences you have survived highlight the importance of healing old wounds to stop them from overshadowing your present and future. In embracing your journey of healing attachment issues, you can begin to rewrite your stories, focusing on growth and the potential for deeper emotional bonds. In the next chapter, we will explore various techniques to become conscious of your attachment-fueled behaviors.

04.

Emotional Alchemy—Turning Attachment-Driven Reactions into Conscious Responses

ITaking time to reflect opens the door to conscious awareness, which brings with it the possibility of change. –Daniel J. Siegel

❝

Understanding the Link Between Attachment Styles and Nervous System Responses

Transforming attachment-driven reactions into conscious responses is an enlightening journey that taps into the depths of your emotional experiences. At its heart, this process involves recognizing how your ingrained patterns and past attachments impact your present interactions. By understanding these dynamics, you open a door to personal growth, offering a pathway to more mindful living.

Attachment styles are deeply intertwined with the nervous system's behavior. Steven Porges's polyvagal theory offers a groundbreaking framework for understanding how these attachment-driven reactions manifest (Polyvagal Theory: Advancing the Understanding of the Autonomic Nervous System, 2023). For starters, your autonomic nervous system, comprising the sympathetic and parasympathetic branches, determines how you react to various situations, whether through stress-induced fight-or-flight responses or moments of calm and connection. The relatively newer ventral vagal complex, unique to mammals, is integral in shaping your social engagements, emotional regulation, and, ultimately, your attachment styles.

The beauty of the polyvagal theory lies in its explanation of how attachment styles influence our autonomic nervous patterns. These patterns, molded by our early attachment experiences, affect not only how we relate to others but also how our bodies instinctively respond to emotional triggers. Understanding this connection can be transformative for personal growth and emotional healing.

Each style—secure, anxious, avoidant, or disorganized—elicits specific physiological responses during social interactions (Brown McCormick, 2024). Secure attachment often results in a higher ventral vagal tone, promoting social engagement and emotional balance. On the other hand, insecure attachments may be characterized by dysregulated autonomic responses, such as heightened anxiety or avoidance, influencing both our emotional awareness and interpersonal relationships (Brown McCormick, 2024).

Imagine an individual with an anxious attachment style. In social settings, their body might naturally lean toward a state of hyperarousal, triggering a flood of stress hormones and preparing them for possible rejection or abandonment. Conversely, someone with an avoidant attachment might experience hypoarousal, leading their nervous system to shut down emotions to protect against intimacy and vulnerability. These ingrained responses profoundly affect our emotional well-being and ability to connect with others.

Yet, there is hope and empowerment in understanding these mechanisms. Recognizing these bodily reactions as part of our attachment narrative allows us to gain clarity on why we behave instinctively in certain ways. For instance, knowing that your heart races not necessarily because of imminent danger, but due to a learned response from past attachment experiences, can shift your perspective and initiate a process of conscious change.

However, acknowledging the impact of your attachment styles on nervous system regulation doesn't end with recognition. It opens up avenues for altering your instinctive behaviors. By embracing the insights provided by the polyvagal theory, you can work toward soothing your autonomic nervous system, facilitating more mindful and conscious interactions. Simple practices like deep breathing, which engages the ventral vagal complex, can help you achieve a sense of safety and connection, countering the immediate fight-or-flight impulse.

Moreover, understanding these physiological reactions linked to attachment experiences reveals your instinctive behaviors' underlying truths. It provides an opportunity to unpack your habitual patterns, offering a clearer comprehension of your emotional responses. This awareness becomes the stepping stone to intentional, conscious choices in how you respond to the world around you—not out of conditioned reflexes but informed awareness.

Tailored Emotional Regulation Techniques for Different Attachments

When it comes to transforming impulsive reactions into conscious responses, recognizing and working with one's attachment style can be a profound tool. Understanding that emotional regulation techniques vary depending on these styles allows you to tailor your approaches more effectively. Let's delve into specific strategies suited for different attachment styles.

Grounding Techniques

Individuals with anxious attachment often experience intense emotional reactions. This reaction tends to create a strong urge for immediate attention. Those with this attachment style typically have a deep-seated need for closeness and approval from others. When they feel like these needs are not being met, it can lead to significant feelings of anxiety. This makes it essential to find ways to manage these feelings and maintain a sense of balance in relationships.

Grounding exercises play a crucial role in helping manage anxiety related to attachment. These exercises work by helping individuals redirect their focus away from overwhelming thoughts to the present moment. The goal is to create a calming sensation that eases anxiety. Grounding techniques are simple yet effective strategies that anyone can use. They encourage mindfulness and can help center someone's thoughts and feelings, making emotional responses more manageable.

One effective grounding technique involves sensory exploration: the 5-4-3-2-1 technique. It encourages individuals to engage their senses in a structured way. This can be done by identifying five things that they can see. For example, someone might spot a colorful painting on the wall, a bright flower outside, a clock ticking, a computer screen, or a cup of coffee. Focusing on these visual elements can help to anchor thoughts and pull them back into the present.

After identifying things to see, the next step is to find four things you can touch. This could include feeling the texture of clothing, the smooth surface of a desk, the softness of a pillow, or the coolness of a metal object. Engaging with what is physically present helps to ground the individual even further and can create a sense of realness in moments of distress. Next, it is useful to identify three sounds you can hear. This might be the rustle of leaves outside, distant traffic, a ticking clock, or voices from another room. Taking in these auditory details allows for a connection to the surrounding environment and can pull attention away from anxious thoughts.

Then, focus on two smells. This could be the fresh scent of coffee brewing, the smell of a favorite food cooking, or even the fragrance of flowers. Identifying smells helps engage a powerful sense that can trigger positive memories, promoting more calming emotions. Finally, end with one thing you can taste. This might involve sipping on a drink, chewing gum, or even enjoying a small piece of candy. Concentrating on taste provides closure to the sensory exercise and deepens the engagement with the moment.

These grounding techniques can help create a sense of stability and safety. By focusing on sensory experiences, individuals can better manage their emotions, especially in moments of high stress. This practice can be developed over time and does not require special tools or complicated steps.

Introspection to Identify Avoidance Behaviors

Avoidant attachment is a style that often leads individuals to pull away emotionally when they feel threatened in their relationships. This behavior generally stems from a deep-seated fear of losing your independence or an overwhelming desire to protect yourself from intimacy. You may struggle to connect with others on a deeper level, and instead of confronting your feelings, you might choose to withdraw, which can create a barrier to forming meaningful relationships. Recognizing this pattern is the first step in breaking free from the cycle of emotional detachment.

Acknowledging these defense mechanisms is essential. Self-reflection allows you to understand your feelings and the reasons behind your actions. It can be intimidating to face these emotions, but it is a necessary process for personal growth. Learning to observe and analyze one's behaviors creates an opportunity to change and improve relationships. Without this reflective practice, you may remain stuck in patterns of avoidance, unable to appreciate the benefits of emotional intimacy.

One effective way to foster self-reflection is through journaling. This tool can serve as a safe space for you to express your thoughts and feelings. Writing can ease the burden of emotional processing and provide clarity. For instance, taking time each day to jot down feelings about interactions with others can help reveal underlying fears or insecurities. Journaling encourages you to articulate your experiences, leading to insights that may not be obvious during day-to-day life.

Within the journaling process, asking specific questions can guide reflections. Useful questions might include: "What am I avoiding in this relationship?" or "How does distancing myself serve me, and what might it cost in terms of connection?" Such questions challenge you to think about your responses and behaviors critically. They provide an opportunity to explore the reasoning behind your actions and the potential impact on your relationships.

Multifaceted Approach to Respond to Disorganized Attachment

Individuals with disorganized attachment often display a mix of behaviors typically associated with anxious and avoidant attachment styles. They might seek closeness and intimacy, yet simultaneously push others away, creating a push-pull dynamic in their relationships. For example, someone might eagerly engage with a partner one moment and then withdraw the next, leaving both them and their partner confused and frustrated. This conflict can stem from a deep-seated fear of rejection or abandonment that coexists with a desire for connection.

To help manage the emotional chaos that can arise from disorganized attachment, individuals can adopt a combination of techniques that draw from both anxious and avoidant strategies. For example, grounding exercises such as deep breathing, focusing on physical sensations, or engaging with the immediate environment can be a powerful first step in this process.

Once individuals have begun to feel a sense of calm through grounding exercises, they can transition to reflective journaling. Over time, this practice can help create a more coherent emotional narrative, where conflicting feelings are acknowledged and can coexist without overwhelming the individual.

Engaging with a professional, such as a therapist, can greatly enhance this process. Therapy offers a structured environment where you can explore your attachment styles and emotional complexities with the guidance of someone knowledgeable. A therapist can help you understand your behaviors and patterns in a safe setting, facilitating deeper insight and healing. They might use various therapeutic techniques, such as cognitive behavioral therapy or attachment-focused therapy, which can provide tools for managing emotions and developing healthier perspectives on relationships.

One key aspect of addressing disorganized attachment is learning emotional regulation. This means being able to manage one's emotions effectively, especially during times of stress or conflict. For this, you might practice mindfulness techniques, which encourage a nonjudgmental awareness of thoughts and feelings. This can help in recognizing emotional triggers and developing healthier responses. For instance, when feeling overwhelmed, you might take a moment to breathe deeply and remind yourself that you can take control of your reactions.

Embracing the complexity of emotional experiences is a vital part of healing from disorganized attachment. It's important to realize that having mixed feelings is normal and doesn't have to lead to conflict. For instance, feeling both love and fear in a relationship is something many people experience. Accepting these emotions as part of being human can build self-compassion and understanding. Ultimately, approaching relationships with this mindset can help you navigate your connections with greater ease and resilience.

CHAPTER 4

Personalization Techniques

The process of personalization through experimentation offers a dynamic way to build unique emotional regulation toolkits. Each person's journey toward emotional regulation will differ, and finding what works best for you requires a willingness to try various methods. Inspired by cognitive-behavioral techniques, individuals can experiment with mindfulness practices, such as meditation or breath work, alongside more active methods like physical exercise or creative expression. Keeping a "regulation diary" can track which methods work in different situations, leading to a customized toolkit tailored to individual needs. This empowerment through choice and creativity nurtures a deeper self-awareness and enhances one's ability to respond consciously.

Recognizing the discomfort that arises in stressful relationship situations is integral to this process. For instance, being attuned to signals of tension or unease prompts timely engagement with regulation techniques before reactions spiral. You should be encouraged to identify coping mechanisms that align with your attachment-driven responses, nurturing a healthier emotional landscape.

Moreover, engaging in self-compassion during automatic reactions becomes a key theme across all attachment styles. It's important to remember that these patterns are deeply ingrained and often stem from past experiences. Being gentle and patient with yourself throughout this transformative process promotes growth. Regularly practice things like reciting affirmations or compassionate introspections to remind yourself that struggling with intense or complex emotions is part of being human and that everyone is on a unique path of healing and development.

Practicing Emotional Flexibility to Cultivate Thoughtful Responses

Emotional flexibility is a cornerstone in navigating complex human relationships. It refers to the ability to sense, interpret, and adjust one's emotional reactions across varying contexts, which allows you to maintain equilibrium and resilience when faced with challenging situations or diverse interpersonal interactions (Koydemir, n.d.). Embracing emotional flexibility can be particularly transformative if you struggle with impulsive reactions driven by attachment styles, as it empowers a shift toward more mindful and intentional responses. Here are practical strategies to help you enhance emotional flexibility.

Understand Emotional Flexibility

To develop emotional flexibility, it is important to start with a clear understanding of what emotional flexibility means. At its essence, emotional flexibility refers to the ability to recognize and understand your feelings while adjusting your reactions based on the context. This skill allows individuals to be aware of their emotions and to manage those emotions in a way that is constructive. For example, if you feel anger in a situation, instead of reacting immediately, emotional flexibility encourages you to recognize that anger, take a moment to think, and find a response that suits the situation better.

Instead of responding impulsively, emotional flexibility involves taking a step back and reflecting on what you're feeling. For example, if someone gives you critical feedback at work, rather than reacting defensively or shutting down, emotional flexibility prompts you to pause, assess why you feel hurt, and decide on the best way to address the feedback. This reflection can lead to more productive conversations and allow you to learn from the experience.

Aligning Responses with Values

Emotional flexibility also means being able to align your responses with your personal values and goals. Understanding your core values is crucial. For instance, if you value kindness, then in a conflict, you might choose a response that maintains your reputation for being considerate. This could mean taking a moment to respond peacefully rather than reactively.

When you adapt your emotional responses in this way, you strengthen your relationships with others while staying true to yourself. Knowing what truly matters to you can guide your responses. Create a list of your core values, such as honesty, family, friendship, or success. When faced with a challenging emotional situation, refer to this list. Ask yourself how your response can align with these values. This strategy will help ensure that your reactions are consistent with who you want to be.

Mindful Practices to Cultivate Emotional Flexibility

A practical exercise that you can do at home or whenever you have five minutes to spare is the recognition of your bodily sensations related to attachment responses. By paying attention to physical cues—such as the tightness in your chest, your racing heart, or tension in your shoulders—you gain insight into your emotional states. Awareness of these sensations acts as an early warning system, reminding you to pause and assess rather than react reflexively. Techniques like breath work or grounding exercises can be particularly useful in these moments, serving as quick and effective tools to regain composure and achieve emotional adaptability.

Developing emotional flexibility also involves building empathy toward others. When you are aware of your own feelings, it becomes easier to understand the emotions of those around you. Try to put yourself in someone else's shoes during conversations, especially in conflicts. This practice can help you respond in ways that consider the emotions of others, leading to more compassionate interactions.

Learning From Mistakes and Seeking

Continuous Growth

Lastly, embrace mistakes as learning experiences. When you find that you didn't respond ideally in a situation, instead of beating yourself up, analyze why it happened. Ask yourself what you were feeling at that moment and what you could do differently next time. For example, if you reacted with frustration during a disagreement, think about what triggered your reaction and how you could manage your feelings more effectively in a similar situation in the future. Learning from each experience will gradually build your emotional flexibility.

Developing emotional flexibility is not a one-time effort but a continuous journey. As you learn and grow, you will find that your emotional responses become more aligned with your values and goals. Gradually, the time you take to pause and reflect will become a natural part of your emotional toolkit. Each small step you take toward increasing your emotional flexibility leads to healthier interactions, better conflict management, and overall improved emotional well-being.

Seeking Support

Creating supportive environments is another key component in enhancing openness and encouraging emotional expression. When surrounded by empathetic and nonjudgmental individuals, people feel safer expressing their true emotions and explore new ways of responding. Supportive environments act as incubators for emotional growth, offering encouragement as you practice new emotional skills.

Getting feedback from friends or family can also enhance your emotional flexibility. They can offer perspectives on how they perceive your emotional reactions. If a friend tells you that you often seem abrupt when you're stressed, this can help you recognize the need for adjustment. Ask for specific examples of your emotional reactions so that you can learn from them and work on improvement.

Additionally, role-playing different scenarios can be a useful exercise. Practice with a trusted friend or family member. Act out situations where you typically struggle emotionally. This rehearsal can help you explore various ways to respond to those triggers. Over time, this strategy can equip you with better responses, making it easier to adjust your emotions when faced with real situations.

Cultivating these environments requires building connections based on trust and respect, where honest communication is encouraged, and each person supports the other's emotional journey. Building such environments can take place in everyday settings, such as within family units or friend circles, or more structured settings like support groups or therapy sessions.

Interactive Exercise

Pause-and-Reflect

It can be easy to react impulsively without fully considering your thoughts and feelings. This exercise is designed to help you cultivate a structured pausing technique that enhances reflection and improves the quality of your relational responses. By taking a moment to pause and reflect, you can respond more thoughtfully in conversations, leading to deeper connections and understanding.

The three-step pause-and-reflect technique can be practiced anywhere, anytime, and during any conversation. Simply follow these steps to mindfully assess your thoughts and feelings:

1. **Pause**: When you find yourself in a conversation or situation that triggers an emotional response, take a moment to pause. Close your eyes, take a deep breath, and count to five. This brief pause allows you to step back from your immediate feelings.

2. **Reflect**: In your mind, ask yourself three questions: Spend a minute reflecting on these questions. This process helps clarify your emotions and intentions.

    - *What am I feeling right now?*

    - *Why do I feel this way?*

    - *How might my response affect the other person?*

3. **Respond**: After reflecting, choose a response that aligns with your feelings and promotes healthy communication. Share your thoughts or feelings with the other person in a calm and constructive manner.

This exercise can be practiced in everyday situations—whether during a conversation with a friend, a challenging discussion at work, or even while driving in traffic. Whenever you sense a strong emotional reaction, remember to pause, reflect, and respond. By incorporating this technique into your interactions, you will foster more meaningful relationships and improve your communication skills.

PAUSE-AND-REFLECT

_____

_____

_____

_____

_____

_____

_____

In this chapter, we've journeyed through the intricate link between attachment styles and our nervous system responses. We've seen how understanding these connections can transform impulsive reactions into mindful, conscious responses. By exploring techniques tailored to different attachment styles—whether through grounding exercises for anxious hearts or reflective practices for avoidant souls—we've provided a roadmap for emotional regulation. The goal is not just to recognize what drives us but to harness this awareness to shape healthier, more intentional responses.

Remember that cultivating emotional flexibility is essential for personal growth and healing. It's about pausing, reflecting, and choosing responses aligned with deeper values rather than automatic reflexes. As you turn over the page, you will learn different strategies to develop a secure attachment and nurture healthy relationships with others.

05.

Building Secure Relationships in a World of Insecure Patterns

When we make our original blueprint more conscious, we can actually help ourselves heal and regain healthy attachment patterns that will benefit us for the rest of our lives. Even if we didn't grow up with secure attachment, we can learn it later. –Diane Poole Heller

❝

Characteristics of Secure Attachment Behaviors

Building secure relationships in a world marked by insecure patterns is an endeavor grounded in awareness and intentionality. At the heart of these secure connections lies the ability to communicate openly and constructively, a skill that can transform interactions from misinterpreted messages to mutual understanding.

Understanding the traits and behaviors of securely attached individuals can provide valuable insights into how one can cultivate healthier relationships. These characteristics form a kind of blueprint for building secure bonds, starting with open and constructive communication.

Open and Healthy Communication

Securely attached individuals have a special skill when it comes to communicating their needs. They express themselves clearly and in a way that allows for constructive conversations. This effective style of communication helps to strengthen understanding between people. When both parties understand each other, it minimizes misunderstandings that can often lead to conflicts.

CHAPTER 5

Moreover, these individuals engage in conversations with empathy, which means they are considerate of the other person's feelings. They do not just talk about themselves; they also listen actively to others. During discussions, they pay attention to what their partner is saying and show that they value their thoughts. This two-way dialogue is essential because it ensures that both individuals feel heard and appreciated, which promotes a cooperative atmosphere in the relationship.

For example, when a securely attached person and their partner are resolving conflict, they might approach it in a calm and thoughtful manner. Instead of blaming each other or simply stating what they want, they might say, "I feel disconnected from you lately; can we sit down and figure out a solution together?" This kind of statement is not only clear but also opens the door for further discussion. It allows both people to express their thoughts without feeling attacked or defensive.

When someone uses this method of communication, they are being transparent about their feelings. They are sharing their emotions instead of hiding them. This type of openness is key for strong relationships. It encourages the other person to share their feelings as well, which creates a more balanced exchange.

Challenge yourself:

1. Take time to understand your own thoughts and feelings before engaging in conversations with others.

2. Focus fully on the speaker, avoiding interruptions, and show that you value their perspective through nods or verbal affirmations.

3. Designate specific times to discuss important topics, ensuring both parties are mentally prepared.

4. Encourage deeper conversations by asking questions that require more than just a yes or no answer.

5. After discussions, summarize what you've understood to ensure clarity and mutual agreement.

6. After difficult conversations, check in later to reaffirm mutual understanding and strengthen the relationship.

Emotional Availability

Emotional availability is a key characteristic of secure attachment in relationships. Securely attached individuals can recognize and respond to their partners' emotional needs. They have the ability to see when their partner is feeling down or anxious and provide the necessary support. This responsiveness fosters a sense of safety in the relationship. When partners feel supported, they can openly share their feelings without worrying about being judged or dismissed.

A good example of emotional availability can be seen in how partners interact during tough times. Let's consider a situation where one partner is stressed due to work pressures. The securely attached partner notices their discomfort and approaches the situation with care. They might start by simply asking, "How was your day?" This question opens the door for the stressed partner to share their feelings. The securely attached partner listens attentively, nodding and making eye contact to show that they are engaged in the conversation.

Validating emotional experiences is also crucial in these moments. If the stressed partner expresses frustration about their workload, the securely attached individual might respond with phrases like, "That sounds really challenging," or, "I can see how that would be overwhelming." Such responses help the stressed partner feel understood. It's important to confirm the partner's feelings, making them feel seen and heard. This validation is not just about agreeing but sharing a space where the partner feels it's okay to vent.

Moreover, being emotionally available does not mean that one partner must solve the other's problems. Rather, it's about being there to help carry the emotional weight together. For example, if the stressed partner is worried about an upcoming deadline, the securely attached partner does not jump in with solutions like, "Just do this," or, "You should talk to your boss." Instead, they might say, "I'm here for you. Let's talk it through." This approach provides an opportunity for the stressed partner to think aloud and process their feelings.

In a supportive environment, both partners can reveal vulnerabilities without fear. This safe space encourages healthy communication. For instance, if the stressed partner feels they have made mistakes at work, they might express feelings of inadequacy. The securely attached partner can remind them, "Everyone makes mistakes, and it's normal.

What's important is what you learn from it." This statement helps in further validating their experience while gently guiding them back to a healthier perspective. Creating an emotional safety net helps partners navigate tough times together. Being responsive to emotional cues does not only enhance understanding but also promotes collaboration in problem-solving.

Challenge yourself:

1. Set aside time each week to write about your emotional experiences and then share the insights with each other, promoting deeper understanding and connection.

2. Implement a daily or weekly ritual where you both ask each other specific questions about your feelings, such as, "What made you feel happy today?" or, "What stressed you out?"

3. Engage in role-reversal exercises where you express your partner's feelings and they express yours, allowing for a deeper understanding of each other's emotional world.

4. Collaboratively develop a list of emotions with descriptions and examples to help identify and articulate feelings more precisely during conversations.

5. Develop unique rituals that signal emotional availability, such as a special hand gesture, phrase, or a safe word that lets your partner know you're ready to listen.

6. Read books on emotional intelligence together and discuss how the themes apply to your relationship, providing a shared context for emotional growth.

7. When faced with decisions, invite each other to express how different choices make you feel, emphasizing the importance of emotional input in decision-making.

8. At the end of each day, share three things you appreciated about each other's emotional support, reinforcing positive behaviors and emotional availability.

Confidence in the Strength of the Relationship

Confidence in a relationship is built on two main pillars: trust and reliability. When partners trust each other, they feel secure in their bond. This sense of security comes from knowing that their partner is dependable. For example, if one partner consistently shows up when they say they will, it creates a strong foundation of trust. This trust allows them to engage in the relationship more fully. They do not spend their time worrying about whether their partner will be there emotionally or physically. Instead, they can focus on enjoying their time together and building a deeper connection.

Securely attached individuals are often characterized by their belief in the consistency of their partners. They feel confident that their partners will act in ways that reinforce the strength of their bond. This belief helps to create a stable environment where both people can thrive. For instance, imagine a couple that has been together for a few years. They have established routines and mutual expectations that contribute to their sense of reliability. When one partner knows that the other will be there to support them during tough times, it encourages them to open up more and express their feelings without fear.

This confidence builds a sense of stability within a relationship. When partners feel stable, they do not experience as much anxiety over potential separations or disagreements. This reduced anxiety is vital because it allows individuals to deal with conflicts more productively. They can focus on resolving issues instead of worrying about the state of their relationship. For example, in a disagreement, a securely attached person is likely to discuss their feelings openly instead of resorting to defensive behavior. They understand that conflicts can be resolved without endangering their connection.

Moreover, this confidence empowers partners to give each other the space they need. It helps them recognize that distance does not mean that they are drifting apart. Instead, time apart can be seen as an opportunity for personal growth. One partner might need to travel for work frequently, which can challenge a relationship. However, a securely attached partner sees this situation as a chance to support their loved one's career while maintaining their bond. They trust that their partner's work commitments do not diminish their feelings for each other. This perspective allows both partners to pursue individual interests without requiring constant reassurance.

Challenge yourself:

1. Create a shared vision board that represents goals and dreams as a couple, encouraging teamwork and mutual support for each other's ambitions.

2. Engage in a monthly "date night" challenge where each partner takes turns planning a surprise outing or activity, fostering spontaneity and connection.

3. Write each other handwritten notes expressing appreciation and love, leaving them in unexpected places as a tangible reminder of commitment.

4. Volunteer together for a cause that resonates with both partners, deepening the bond through shared experiences and values.

5. Set aside time to learn a new skill or hobby together, reinforcing teamwork and enjoyment of each other's company in a fun, relaxed setting.

6. Initiate a "no-technology" evening once a week, allowing for focused, quality time that strengthens connection and presence.

7. Create a couple's book club where both partners read the same book and discuss it, building intellectual and emotional intimacy through shared insights.

Interest in Personal Growth

A commitment to personal growth is essential for healthy and secure attachments in relationships. This means that individuals actively strive to improve themselves, which in turn benefits their connections with others. When people focus on their growth, they are more likely to approach challenges with a positive mindset. Instead of seeing obstacles as something negative, they view them as opportunities. For example, if a couple faces a disagreement, rather than allowing it to create distance, they can see it as a chance to understand each other better.

To embrace challenges effectively, individuals should adopt a mindset that looks for lessons in every situation. When faced with a problem, they can ask themselves questions like, "What can I learn from this?" or "How can I handle this differently next time?" This approach is incredibly useful in relationships, as it encourages open communication and shared growth. Couples might find it helpful to talk about the challenges they face and how they can learn together. For instance, after an argument, they could discuss what triggered the disagreement and how to manage similar situations better in the future.

Seeking new experiences is another way to enhance relationship dynamics. Trying new activities together can help couples bond and discover more about each other. This might involve taking up a hobby, traveling to a new place, or simply exploring different restaurants. New experiences create a sense of adventure and can reignite the spark in a relationship. For example, a couple could decide to take a cooking class together. Not only will they learn new skills, but they will also cultivate teamwork and create lasting memories in the process.

Self-reflection plays a crucial role in personal growth. It involves looking inward to understand one's thoughts, feelings, and behaviors. Individuals can set aside time regularly to assess their emotions and actions within the relationship. This practice can help them recognize patterns and areas for improvement. For instance, someone might notice that they often react defensively during discussions. By reflecting on this behavior, they can work on becoming more open and supportive, leading to healthier interactions with their partner.

Challenge yourself:

1. Engage in a monthly "growth date" where each partner shares a book, podcast, or article they've found inspiring, followed by a discussion on its relevance to their relationship.

2. Create a gratitude jar where both partners regularly add notes of appreciation for each other, fostering positivity and connection.

3. Set mutual goals for personal development, like completing a fitness challenge together or taking a class on emotional intelligence.

4. Start a relationship journal that partners rotate writing in, allowing each individual to express thoughts and feelings they may struggle to articulate verbally.

5. Designate a "feedback hour" once a month to discuss what's working or not in the relationship, focusing on constructive criticism and solutions.

Building Trust with Anxious and Avoidant Partners

In building trust with partners who display anxious or avoidant attachment styles, consistency, and predictability play crucial roles. Imagine trying to navigate a maze without a map; this uncertainty breeds anxiety and could lead a partner with an anxious attachment style to constantly feel on edge. Here are practical ways to build and nurture trust with partners who have an anxious or avoidant style of attachment.

Strive to Be Consistent

In any relationship, maintaining consistent behaviors can play a crucial role in its success. One of the key aspects of this is regular communication. Communicating often helps both partners feel connected and informed about each other's thoughts and feelings. This is especially important for anxious and avoidant partners who may be more suspicious or have doubts about their partners' intentions.

For instance, setting aside time each week for a phone call or a chat can create a routine that brings both partners closer. This dedicated time can be used to discuss issues, share updates, or simply enjoy casual conversation. When partners make communication a priority, it lays a strong foundation for trust and understanding.

Another important behavior when being in a relationship with an anxious or avoidant individual is keeping your promises. When you commit to something, whether it is something small or significant, following through matters. If you promise to attend an important event, make every effort to be there. This consistent reliability builds trust over time. If one partner often breaks promises or shows unreliability, the other may feel anxious or uncertain about the future of the relationship. In contrast, if both partners see that they can depend on each other, it cultivates an environment where they feel safe to share their thoughts and emotions.

Predictability is another benefit of consistent behaviors. When one partner is able to predict the actions of the other, it helps to reduce anxiety. Anxious or avoidant partners may struggle with fear of the unknown; therefore, when behaviors are consistent, it creates a sense of stability. For instance, if one partner always responds to texts within a few minutes, the other partner will learn to expect that. This predictability can lessen the worries that sometimes come with uncertainty, as individuals can anticipate their partner's actions and reactions. As a result, the relationship feels more secure and grounded.

Creating Safe Spaces for Meaningful Dialogue

Creating a safe space for dialogue is vital when nurturing relationships, especially with partners who may be anxious or avoidant. A safe space is an environment where both partners feel comfortable sharing their thoughts and feelings without fear of judgment or criticism. This kind of atmosphere encourages vulnerability, which is crucial for building deeper connections. It allows individuals to express themselves honestly, leading to more understanding and compassion between partners.

Vulnerability is the willingness to expose one's thoughts and emotions. In a relationship, it's essential because it helps both partners know each other on a deeper level. When one person shares their fears, hopes, or concerns, it opens the door for the other partner to respond with empathy. For example, if one partner shares anxiety about future plans, the other might reassure them by discussing their own feelings or by suggesting ways they can manage that anxiety together. This kind of exchange strengthens the relationship by creating a bond of trust.

CHAPTER 5

Creating a safe space does not mean avoiding difficult conversations. On the contrary, these conversations can be very beneficial when handled correctly. It is important to approach these discussions respectfully and empathetically. This means listening actively, validating feelings, and expressing one's thoughts without becoming defensive. For instance, if a partner brings up an issue that is bothering them, the other partner should take the time to listen fully before responding. They might say, "I hear you, and I want to understand more about how you feel." This approach shows that they care about their partner's feelings and are willing to work through challenges together.

One effective way to promote transparency and build trust over time is to set aside dedicated time each week for open conversations about relationship matters. Having a regular check-in allows both partners to express their feelings and discuss any issues that may have arisen. It could be a simple ritual, such as a Friday evening dinner or a Sunday morning coffee date, where the focus is solely on each other and their relationship. This time should be free of distractions, like phones or TV, creating an atmosphere where both partners can be present and attentive to each other.

Showing Patience

Patience is a vital quality that can greatly influence the dynamics of a relationship, especially when one partner shows insecure attachment patterns. Giving your partner the grace and time needed to adjust to your relationship is fundamental. This might mean allowing them to express their feelings at their own pace, rather than rushing them into open conversations about trust or vulnerability. For instance, if your partner seems hesitant to share personal thoughts, try not to press them too hard. Instead, create a safe space for them to share when they feel ready.

Setbacks are a normal part of any relationship, especially one that involves insecure attachment styles. It's important to understand that these setbacks do not signify failure. They are more like bumps in the road. For example, if your partner withdraws or reacts negatively to a discussion, recognize that it might stem from their past experiences, and not from a lack of love for you. Showing understanding in these moments can significantly strengthen your bond.

As you practice patience, it's equally important to celebrate the small victories along the way. Each time your partner opens up or shares their needs or feelings, it is a step forward. Acknowledge these moments. You might say something like, "I really appreciate you sharing that with me," or, "It means a lot to hear your thoughts." Celebrating these small milestones encourages your partner and reinforces trust.

These small victories are crucial because they build a foundation for more significant changes in the relationship. Each positive interaction can help convince your partner that they can trust you. Over time, this consistent reinforcement will help them feel safer and more secure. For example, if your partner starts discussing their feelings more often, that's a positive sign that they are becoming more comfortable with vulnerability.

During tough times, your commitment can shine through. When challenges arise, it's easy to feel discouraged. However, staying dedicated during these moments shows that you genuinely care about the relationship. Be present for your partner. Talk with them about their feelings, listen actively, and validate their emotions. You might find that simply being there can provide the comfort and security your partner needs.

Finally, the journey to establish strong bonds through patience involves acknowledging that healing takes time. Anxious or avoidant partners might initially exhibit distrust due to prior experiences. Be patient as they learn to navigate this new relational landscape. Communicate your intentions clearly and consistently, reassuring them through actions rather than words alone. If, after several attempts, progress feels stagnant, consider seeking external guidance, like therapy, which can provide tailored strategies for navigating complex attachment dynamics.

Breaking Toxic Cycles and Understanding Security as a Process

Building secure relationships in a world filled with insecurity is no small feat. Understanding and breaking the vicious cycles that so often plague relationships can be transformative. To start, it's crucial to identify destructive patterns within your relationships. These patterns are negative loops that, once recognized, offer a roadmap for change. Whether they manifest as repeated arguments about the same old issues or as silent resentments, recognizing these patterns allows you to engage proactively.

Identifying these patterns requires honest self-reflection and sometimes external insights from trusted friends or professionals. For example, if every disagreement escalates into defensiveness instead of dialogue, there's clearly a pattern at play. By acknowledging these behaviors, you create an opportunity to dissect them—uncovering root causes like unmet needs or past experiences influencing current dynamics. When these triggers come to light, partners can work together toward solutions that address core issues rather than merely dealing with symptoms. Unmet needs often cause emotional regressions, resulting in cycles where we continue seeking fulfillment in unproductive or damaging ways (Murauskas, 2023).

Once destructive patterns are laid bare, implementing interruption strategies is the next step on the journey to secure relationships. Strategies like taking a break during tense situations can significantly shift interactions from destructive to constructive. Furthermore, pausing an argument when emotions run high allows both parties space to cool down and reflect, which can prevent escalation and promote more effective communication upon return to the discussion (Zimmerman, 2024). Consider establishing a mutual agreement with your partner to use "timeouts" when dialogues become too heated. During this pause, focus on calming techniques like deep breathing or mindful reflection to gain clarity and calm.

These interruption strategies not only halt negative momentum but also redirect focus onto solutions rather than problems. They pave the way for engaging in repair conversations, which form the essence of long-lasting bonds in relationships. When partners commit to conversations rooted in accountability, they build trust and establish reconciliation habits. In such dialogues, accountability means owning up to one's role in misunderstandings or conflicts without deflecting blame. Engaging genuinely and empathetically encourages openness and vulnerability, essential ingredients in forging strong connections.

A poignant aspect of repair is the willingness to apologize sincerely and seek forgiveness, thereby reinforcing the relationship's foundation. Apologies serve as acknowledgments of the hurt caused and an expression of commitment to personal growth and the relationship itself. It's also vital to express gratitude for the partner's patience and effort in rebuilding trust. This acknowledgment strengthens bonds and establishes a resilient framework for navigating future challenges.

Moving beyond immediate repairs, embracing repair as integral to long-term relationship maintenance is a cornerstone of security. Relationships naturally encounter trials; hence, seeing repair not as a sign of failure but as a natural part of the journey deepens resilience and adaptability. This perspective promotes shared goals for security by encouraging couples to view their relationship as a dynamic entity constantly growing and evolving. Repair becomes less about fixing problems and more about nurturing continuous connection and cooperation.

Securing any relationship involves ongoing efforts and consistent nurturing. It demands that partners continuously invest time in understanding and addressing each other's emerging needs and concerns. Establishing new routines and rituals can support this process by providing structure and predictability, allowing both partners to feel valued and heard consistently. Regular check-ins or date nights dedicated to reconnecting can reaffirm bonds and mitigate feelings of neglect or disconnection that might otherwise arise over time.

Interactive Exercise

Relationship Audit for Assessing Security Levels

Assessing the security of your relationships is crucial for building healthy connections and ensuring that both partners feel valued and understood. Conducting a relationship audit can help you identify areas of strength and opportunities for growth. This guided template will encourage open communication and reflection, allowing you to evaluate your relationship dynamics comprehensively.

Step 1: Rate Your Relationship Using a Scale From 1-10

Reflect on the following aspects of your relationship and rate each on a scale of 1 to 10, with 1 being the lowest and 10 being the highest.

1. Communication: How effectively do you and your partner share thoughts and feelings?

2. Trust: How much do you trust each other with personal matters?

3. Support: How well do you provide emotional and physical support to one another?

4. Conflict Resolution: How do you handle disagreements and conflicts?

5. Quality Time: How much time do you spend together, and how meaningful is it?

6. Intimacy: How satisfied are you with the physical and emotional intimacy in your relationship?

Step 2: Identify Strengths and Weaknesses

Based on your ratings, jot down one strength and one weakness for each aspect.

- **Communication:**
    - Strength:
    - Weakness:
- **Trust:**
    - Strength:
    - Weakness:
- **Support:**
    - Strength:
    - Weakness:
- **Conflict Resolution:**
    - Strength:
    - Weakness:
- **Quality Time:**
    - Strength:
    - Weakness:
- **Intimacy:**
    - Strength:
    - Weakness:

Step 3: Set Goals for Growth

Choose one weakness from each category that you would like to address. Set a specific goal for improvement and note how you can achieve it.

Communication Goal:

Trust Goal:

Support Goal:

Conflict Resolution Goal:

Quality Time Goal:

Intimacy Goal:

Step 4: Discuss Findings

Schedule a time to discuss your findings and goals with your partner. Approach the conversation with openness and a willingness to listen.

Step 5: Revisit Your Audit Regularly

Commit to revisiting this audit every few months to monitor your progress. Adjust your goals as needed and celebrate your achievements together!

Characteristics of secure attachment behaviors serve as both guideposts and inspirations, illustrating how trust, reliability, and emotional availability become the bedrock upon which healthy relationships are built.

They demonstrate how secure attachment nurtures both individual and collective growth by balancing closeness and independence while respecting boundaries. Securely attached individuals navigate emotions and life challenges with resilience, using obstacles as opportunities for connection rather than conflict.

Moving forward, engaging with partners with anxious or avoidant attachment styles requires conscious effort. Consistency in actions, emotional validation, and creating safe spaces for conversation are vital strategies discussed to build trust. It's about patience and celebrating small victories that pave the path toward security. In the following chapter, you will discover how to establish firm boundaries and communicate them confidently to maintain harmony in your relationships.

Make a Difference with Your Review: Unlock the Power of Helping Others

In helping others, we shall help ourselves, for whatever good we give out completes the circle and comes back to us. –Flora Edwards

❝

Helping others not only feels good but also makes a big difference in the world. That's why I have a special question for you today...

Would you be willing to help someone you've never met, without expecting anything in return?

Imagine someone out there who is just like you used to be—maybe feeling a bit lost, searching for answers, or hoping to create and sustain meaningful relationships. They need guidance, just like you once did.

That's where the *Anxious, Avoidant, and Disorganized Attachment Recovery Workbook* comes into play. My goal is to get this life-changing book into the hands of as many people as possible because I believe in its power to transform lives. But I can't do this alone.

The truth is, many people rely on reviews when deciding whether to invest in a book. So here's my heartfelt request on behalf of a fellow reader you've never met:

Please consider leaving a review for this book.

Your feedback doesn't cost a dime and takes less than a minute to share, but it could profoundly impact someone else's journey toward healing and growth. Your review could be the nudge that helps someone:

- Start their journey of personal healing.
- Discover tools to build healthier relationships.
- Gain the confidence to set boundaries and reclaim their independence.
- Learn techniques that could change their life's path.
- Embark on a transformative personal journey.

Scan the QR code or click this link to leave your review:

☆ ☆ ☆ ☆ ☆

If you feel a spark of joy knowing you could help someone in such a simple yet impactful way, then you're exactly the kind of person I love to connect with. Welcome to the club—you're one of us now!

I'm excited to help you navigate the path to healthier relationships and personal empowerment. You're going to find the strategies and lessons in the upcoming chapters incredibly valuable.

Thank you from the bottom of my heart for your support. Let's return to our journey of growth and learning together.

With gratitude, Lulu Nicholson

P.S. - Remember, when you offer something valuable to someone, you become more valuable in their eyes. If you think this book could help another person like it helped you, consider sharing it with them.

06.

Mastering the Art of Boundaries without Losing Connection

When we fail to set boundaries and hold people accountable, we feel used and mistreated. This is why we sometimes attack who they are, which is far more hurtful than addressing a behavior or a choice. –Brené Brown

❝

Transforming Boundaries from Barriers to Protective Filters

Boundaries often get a bad rap, since they are perceived as walls that isolate rather than connect people (Reid, 2022). Yet, they serve a crucial purpose in not only safeguarding your emotional well-being but also in cultivating healthier, more authentic interactions with others. By reimagining boundaries as flexible tools rather than rigid barriers, you begin to see them as instruments of care for both yourself and those you love.

Boundaries serve as essential protective elements within relationships. They act like invisible shields, safeguarding your emotional health while allowing you to remain open to meaningful connections. By clearly defining these invisible lines, you create a space where you can feel comfortable and supported. Rather than excluding others, boundaries offer an invitation for genuine interaction based on mutual respect (Reid, 2022). When you establish boundaries, you are essentially setting the terms for how you engage with others and how they engage with you.

Consider boundaries as a framework for communication and understanding. In the same way that rules enable games to be played fairly, boundaries provide the necessary structure that allows interactions to flourish. They clarify expectations and reduce misunderstandings, creating an environment conducive to honest dialogue. For instance, if you need uninterrupted time to recharge after work, communicating this boundary to a partner or family member can prevent resentment from building up. In this scenario, a boundary supports a relationship by facilitating clear communication about each person's needs and limits.

The misconception that boundaries equate to rejection is common but misleading. Setting boundaries is not about pushing people away; instead, it signifies a deep level of self-care and respect. By articulating and adhering to your boundaries, you assert your worth and honor your limitations, showing others that you value yourself enough to protect your mental and emotional space. Let's imagine a situation where someone requires alone time after a social gathering. Expressing this need doesn't mean rejecting the company of others; rather, it's a way to ensure the individual remains emotionally available when next engaging socially. Thus, boundaries help maintain one's capacity for connection, ensuring they are fully present when interacting with others.

Understanding the purpose behind boundaries requires acknowledgment that they are meant to support your emotional health. Their flexibility allows for adjustments as circumstances change or evolve. People often fear that boundaries are fixed and impermeable, leading to loneliness and isolation. However, healthy boundaries are adaptable. They shift to accommodate growth, changes in relationships, or new personal insights. This adaptability ensures that relationships remain dynamic and responsive to the needs of everyone involved.

The idea is to view boundaries as part of a balanced approach to personal space and relational openness. Striking this balance means recognizing when to say yes to engagement and when to retreat for self-preservation. It enables you to invest in relationships without losing sight of your emotional needs. When practiced effectively, these boundaries become expressions of love and care both for yourself and others.

CHAPTER 6

Setting Compassionate Yet Firm Boundaries with Loved Ones

Many adults struggle with the balance of being kind while also being assertive. It's a common challenge, especially for those who have faced difficulties in nurturing relationships. The fear of upsetting someone can lead us to avoid difficult conversations. Yet, being kind does not mean sacrificing our needs. It means being honest and respectful toward ourselves and others. So how do we navigate these waters to honor our feelings without hurting someone else's?

A significant factor behind difficulties in setting boundaries is often our attachment styles, which develop in our early relationships. Insecure attachment styles can manifest as anxiety or avoidance in relationships. For instance, someone with an anxious attachment style might fear that expressing their needs will push others away. On the other hand, those with an avoidant attachment style may distance themselves from others, thinking that they don't need anyone else to meet their needs. Recognizing our attachment style is a vital step toward understanding our behavior in relationships and can guide us in making changes.

Crafting Messages with Empathy

One way to establish and maintain healthy boundaries is by utilizing effective communication techniques. One technique is the use of "I" statements. These statements allow you to convey your feelings and needs without blaming others, thus reducing defensiveness and promoting understanding. By initiating conversations with phrases like "I feel" or "I need," you open up a dialogue centered around your emotions, making it easier for others to understand your perspective. For example, instead of saying, "You never listen to me," try saying, "I feel unheard when I speak, and I need your attention." This subtle shift in language encourages empathy and promotes healthier interactions. As such, "I" statements become a valuable tool in maintaining both self-respect and respect for others.

The DESO technique is another effective tool for communication and problem-solving. It stands for Describe, Express, Specify, and Outcome

(Astray, 2020). This technique can help individuals articulate their thoughts and feelings clearly. Each step helps to ensure that the message is conveyed effectively and understood by others.

Describe

The first step in the DESO technique is to describe the situation or issue at hand. This involves providing a clear and straightforward account of what is happening. For example, if you are facing a conflict with a colleague at work, you might start by describing the events that led to the disagreement. You could say, "I noticed that during our last team meeting, my ideas were not acknowledged, and I felt overlooked." It is essential to stick to the facts and avoid making assumptions or judgments. Being specific about the details helps to set the stage for what comes next.

Express

Next, you move on to the Express stage. This is where you share your feelings and emotions related to the situation. It is important to communicate how the described incident has affected you. Continuing with the previous example, you might say, "When my ideas were not acknowledged, I felt frustrated and disheartened." This part allows you to convey your emotional response honestly, making it clear to the listener how the situation has impacted you. Using "I" statements can help prevent the other person from feeling defensive, as it focuses on your experience rather than placing blame.

Specify

Once you have described the situation and expressed your feelings, the next step is Specify. In this stage, you clarify what you need or want from the other person. This is crucial for moving toward a resolution. You might specify by saying, "I would appreciate it if, during our meetings, my ideas could be considered." This clear request gives the listener a concrete understanding of what you are hoping to achieve. By being specific, you provide a clear direction for how the other person can support or collaborate with you.

Outcome

The final step in the DESO technique is the Outcome. This is where you outline the desired outcome or what you hope to achieve moving forward. Here, you can express any expectations you have regarding the situation. For instance, you could say, "I hope that by discussing this, we can enhance our teamwork and ensure everyone feels heard." By sharing your desired outcome, you create a vision for a better future, inviting the other person to engage in the solution.

For practical application, take a moment to reflect on a recent interaction where the DESO technique could be useful. Write down the details of the situation, how it made you feel, what you need from the other person, and what outcome you desire. This written exercise can help clarify your thoughts.

The DESO technique can be applied in various scenarios, whether at work, in friendships, or within families. Consider how you can adapt this method to fit different contexts. For example, if you have a disagreement with a family member about household responsibilities, use the DESO technique to clearly communicate your feelings. Describe the issue, express how it affects you, specify what changes you would like to see, and share your vision for a harmonious living environment.

The Balance of Firmness and Compassion

Understanding that firmness does not mean being aggressive is vital. Assertiveness can be communicated in a gentle yet effective way. This means you can express your needs without being harsh or confrontational. It's important to recognize the difference between being firm and being aggressive. Firmness is about standing your ground while still being respectful, while aggression often comes off as domineering or unfriendly. When you are firm, you can rephrase your needs calmly and stick to them, even if others push back. It's essential to have confidence in the importance of your requests and to present them in a way that encourages open communication instead of conflict.

Think about times when you need to set boundaries, whether it's regarding your time or your emotional energy. Having templates for these situations can be very helpful. For example, if someone is asking for your time and you feel overcommitted, you can say something like, "I appreciate the invitation, but I need some time for myself this weekend." This response is clear and acknowledges the invitation while establishing a boundary for your personal space. Similarly, in situations where emotional support is needed, you could express, "I'm here for you, yet I also need time to process my own emotions." This statement shows that you care for others while also emphasizing your own needs, allowing for a balanced exchange.

Setting boundaries starts with understanding your capacity. Sometimes, people may not realize they are overstepping. By being open about what you can handle, you can foster better relationships. You don't need to feel guilty about needing time alone or requiring emotional space. It's a normal part of maintaining your mental health. You might consider taking a moment to reflect on how much time you realistically have available before committing to activities or supporting others. This allows for a more accurate assessment of your limits.

Practicing firmness involves preparation. You could try rehearsing what you want to say in advance, which can help reduce anxiety when the moment arises. This practice can increase your confidence and make it easier to communicate your boundaries clearly when the time comes. Remember, your feelings and needs are valid, and practicing expressing them can make a significant difference in your interactions. Moreover, look for opportunities to reinforce your boundaries positively.

Complimenting someone when they respect your time or emotional needs can encourage this behavior in the future. For instance, if a friend understands when you need to retreat for some personal time, letting them know accordingly can strengthen your relationship. Expressing gratitude shows that you appreciate their efforts to understand you.

Maintaining consistency is crucial once you have established your boundaries. If you make a decision about your time or emotional energy, stick to it. If you often waver, it can confuse those around you about the seriousness of your boundaries. Clarity leads to respect, not only from others but also from yourself. This involves saying no when necessary and upholding your choices even if it feels uncomfortable at first.

Cultivating Resilience to Pushback

Navigating the reactions of loved ones requires patience and understanding. Your loved ones may initially react with surprise, confusion, or even resistance. When this happens, remain calm and reaffirm your boundary kindly but firmly. You might say, "I understand this is different from what I've done before, but this is important for my well-being." Encourage an open dialogue, allowing space for them to express their feelings. By providing explanations that emphasize the importance of maintaining a healthy balance in the relationship, you can work toward achieving mutual understanding.

Identifying personal boundary needs is key to successful implementation. This involves introspection about past experiences and emotional triggers. Reflect on instances where your boundaries were crossed and assess how it made you feel. Did it lead to resentment or emotional exhaustion? Use these insights to define what is acceptable and what isn't in various aspects of your life. A helpful guideline here is to write down situations where you felt uncomfortable or unfulfilled and consider what boundaries could have mitigated these feelings. This practice not only clarifies your needs but also boosts confidence in communicating them.

Encouraging introspection about past boundary failures can inform future practices. Reflecting on these experiences enables you to recognize patterns and adjust your strategies. Perhaps there was a situation where you didn't articulate your needs clearly, leading to misunderstandings. Use these reflections as learning opportunities. Consider questions like

- What prevented you from asserting yourself?
- How did you feel afterward?

Analyzing these situations helps develop a personal framework for setting stronger boundaries going forward. Remember that connecting boundary setting to personal values enhances clarity and purpose. When your boundaries align with your core beliefs, adhering to them feels more natural and justified.

Role-Playing Exercises for Practicing Boundary Reinforcement

Setting and maintaining healthy boundaries can initially seem like a daunting task, especially when it comes to effectively communicating these boundaries with others. However, by engaging in practical exercises, you can build your confidence and become more adept at reinforcing boundaries in everyday interactions. Role-playing scenarios are an excellent tool for this purpose, providing a safe and structured environment in which you can practice both setting and enforcing boundaries.

Designing relatable role-play exercises is key to making this practice effective. Consider creating scenarios that mirror common boundary-setting situations people often encounter. For instance, one exercise might involve a scenario where a friend constantly borrows items without asking. You would practice articulating a boundary with phrases such as, "I expect you to ask before borrowing my things." Another scenario could involve setting limits on work commitments and practicing how to say no to additional tasks when feeling overburdened. Each of these scenarios helps you explore different aspects of boundary setting in a controlled, low-risk environment, enabling you to experiment with various communication techniques.

Involving friends or peers in these exercises can significantly enhance the learning experience. Practicing with someone familiar can provide valuable feedback and insight into your boundary-setting style. Friends can offer constructive critiques, share personal experiences, and collaboratively brainstorm solutions to overcome any obstacles faced during role-playing sessions. This interactive approach not only nurtures a supportive environment but also encourages open discussions about challenges and successes encountered when setting boundaries in real life.

As you engage in these exercises, it's crucial to incorporate self-assessment questions to evaluate your comfort level and effectiveness in boundary communication. Simple reflective questions can be incredibly insightful. For example, "How did I feel expressing my boundary in this situation?" or, "What can I do differently next time to improve clarity and assertiveness?" These questions help to self-reflect, identify areas for improvement, and reinforce positive techniques learned through practice.

Revisiting Role-Play Challenges

Boundary setting, however, does present certain emotional challenges that can act as barriers to clear communication. A common obstacle is the fear of confrontation, which stems from concerns about damaging relationships or offending others (Boundaries III: Communicating Boundaries, 2023). Emotional responses, such as guilt or anxiety, can also complicate the process of boundary enforcement. To address these hurdles, it's helpful to remind yourself that boundaries are not meant to push people away but to protect your emotional space and promote healthier dynamics. Reframing the mindset around boundaries as tools for connection and respect rather than rejection can alleviate some of the emotional weight associated with their establishment.

Role-playing exercises can explicitly target these emotional responses by offering opportunities to practice in a variety of emotionally charged scenarios. For instance, simulating a conversation with a family member who tends to disregard personal privacy can allow you to prepare for real-life emotional reactions, so you can handle similar situations with greater composure and confidence. Through repeated exposure to these challenging scenarios in a safe environment, you can gradually desensitize yourself to the anxiety of boundary setting and learn to manage your emotions more effectively.

Encouraging an ongoing dialogue with yourself and others about boundary management is vital for personal growth. While role-playing is an excellent starting point, it must be supported by continuous reflection and adaptation. By consistently revisiting and adjusting boundaries based on evolving needs and circumstances, you can ensure that your boundary-setting skills remain relevant and effective. Open conversations with peers about boundary adjustments encourage mutual understanding and create environments where everyone's needs are respected.

Interactive Exercise

Scripts for Expressing Boundary Needs Effectively

Communicating boundary needs effectively in varying contexts is crucial for building healthy relationships. To achieve this, having concrete examples and templates can be immensely beneficial, providing clarity and confidence in discussions that might otherwise feel daunting. Here are some scripts that you can use in different scenarios to express your boundaries confidently:

1. Overtime requests

    a. "I appreciate the offer, but I have prior commitments and cannot take on extra hours this week."

    b. "Thank you for considering me for this project, but I need to maintain a work-life balance and will have to decline."

2. Personal space

    a. "I value our time together, but I also need some time alone to recharge."

    b. "I love being close to you, but I need my own space occasionally to feel balanced."

3. Socializing

    a. "I enjoy our hangouts, but I need to take a break from social activities for a while."

    b. "I appreciate the invites, but I'm not up for going out this weekend."

4. Unsolicited advice

a. "I know you mean well, but I'd prefer to navigate this on my own without advice."

b. "Thank you for your concern, but I would like to make my own decisions."

5. Personal time

a. "I'm dedicated to my work, but I need to unplug after hours to focus on personal projects."

b. "I can ensure productivity during work hours, but I cannot be available outside of those times."

6. Financial decisions

a. "I believe we should discuss major expenses together before making any decisions."

b. "I'm comfortable sharing expenses, but we need to agree on our approach beforehand."

7. Emotional support

a. "I appreciate your support, but I need to process my feelings on my own for now."

b. "I value our friendship, but I can't provide support at this time; I need to focus on myself."

8. Time alone

a. "I love spending time with you, but I need some quiet time to recharge."

b. "I need some time to myself this weekend; I hope you understand."

9. Continuous interruptions

a. "I need to focus on my tasks right now, so I won't be able to chat."

b. "I appreciate the check-ins, but I need uninterrupted time to complete my project."

10. Social media

a. "I prefer to keep some aspects of my life private and stay off social media with our relationship."

b. "I'd rather not post our relationship online; I think it's more special that way."

11. Commitment expectations

a. "I want to be honest, but I can't commit to regular meetups right now."

b. "I cherish our friendship, but I need to keep expectations low to manage my time."

12. Holiday plans

a. "I love our traditions, but I need to spend the holidays differently this year."

b. "I need to prioritize my own family commitments during the holidays, but I hope to join for a meal."

13. Feedback on performance

a. "I welcome constructive feedback, but I'd like to discuss it in a private meeting."

b. "I appreciate input but prefer to receive it scoped specifically to my work."

14. Affection levels

a. "I enjoy being affectionate, but I need us to talk about our comfort levels."

b. "Let's discuss how we express affection so we're both comfortable."

15. Invitations

a. "Thanks for the invite, but I won't be able to make it this time."

b. "I appreciate you thinking of me, but I need to pass on this gathering."

SCRIPTS FOR EXPRESSING BOUNDARY NEEDS EFFECTIVELY

Feel free to expand on this list by crafting your own scripts related to setting boundaries in different aspects of your life.

_____

_____

_____

_____

_____

In this chapter, we have explored how redefining boundaries as flexible tools can strengthen emotional connections and provide safety within your relationships. By shifting your perspective from viewing boundaries as rigid barriers to seeing them as protective filters, you open yourself to healthier interactions grounded in mutual respect.

We've discussed the importance of clear communication in setting these boundaries, emphasizing that they do not signify rejection but are instead acts of self-care. This chapter outlined how boundaries serve as an invitation for genuine conversation, providing the necessary structure so that relationships can flourish without losing sight of your individual needs.

With adaptable boundaries that evolve with changing circumstances, you can maintain dynamic and responsive relationships. As you integrate these insights into your life, remember that boundaries are not just lines drawn; they are bridges built on understanding, ensuring both self-respect and respect for others.

07.

Beyond Communication—Creating Emotional Safety

Psychological safety does not mean that you feel comfortable all the time. Psychological safety means you feel comfortable talking about what makes you uncomfortable. –Esther Derby

"

Differentiating Between Communication and Emotional Safety

In the realm of relationships, effective communication is often lauded as the cornerstone of understanding and connection. However, while communication enables the exchange of information, it frequently falls short of delivering the emotional nuance necessary for a deeper bond. To truly connect with others, one must go beyond surface-level exchanges and strive for emotional safety, which plays an indispensable role in building trust within any relationship.

Communication, at its core, involves the articulation and sharing of thoughts, feelings, and information between individuals. However, words alone can carry varying interpretations based on tone, context, and the listener's emotional state. For instance, a simple phrase like "I'm fine" can signal different emotions depending on the speaker's vocal tone or body language. This highlights the limitation of verbal communication when used in isolation—it may not fully capture or convey the underlying emotions intended by the speaker. This gap creates a need for an environment where individuals feel emotionally secure enough to express their true selves without fear of judgment or reprisal.

Defining Emotional Safety

Emotional safety, unlike mere communication, cultivates a space where vulnerability becomes a shared strength rather than a potential weakness (Matejko, 2021). When partners, family members, or friends feel emotionally safe, they are more likely to open up about their deepest emotions and fears. This openness leads to genuine connections, as both parties engage in an honest and empathetic exchange of feelings. Such an atmosphere encourages individuals to lower their defenses, enabling them to reveal aspects of themselves that they might otherwise keep hidden.

Imagine a scenario where two friends are experiencing conflict. One might choose to communicate by directly stating their grievances, but this approach may lead to defensiveness or misunderstanding if the other friend does not feel emotionally safe. Conversely, if both friends have established an emotionally secure relationship, they are more likely to approach the conversation from a place of empathy and understanding.

Effective communication, when combined with emotional safety, leads to a profound sense of trust and mutual respect. It acknowledges that while clarity in communication is essential, nonverbal cues such as body language, tone, and facial expressions significantly contribute to the message's overall impact. A nod or a gentle smile can communicate understanding and compassion far more effectively than words alone. When individuals feel that their nonverbal expressions are acknowledged in a safe environment, they become more willing to share their emotions openly.

Creating emotional safety is not a passive endeavor; it requires conscious effort and intention. Romantic relationships particularly thrive on emotional safety, as partners learn to navigate each other's emotional landscapes with sensitivity and consideration. For instance, both parties involved must prioritize listening actively, validating each other's feelings, and being mindful of their nonverbal signals. Respecting boundaries and maintaining transparency are also crucial components of this process, as they reinforce trust and reliability over time. When couples commit to these principles, they lay the groundwork for a nurturing environment where authentic connections can flourish.

Take, for example, a couple who regularly shares their hopes and insecurities with each other. Their relationship thrives because they have cultivated an emotionally secure environment where neither feels judged or dismissed. This safety net allows them to explore sensitive topics, address conflicts constructively, and ultimately strengthen their bond. Emotional safety in this context becomes a mutual commitment to understanding and supporting one another unconditionally.

The benefits of integrating emotional safety into communication practices go beyond enhancing individual relationships. It has broader implications for personal growth and healing. In emotionally safe spaces, you can reflect on your past experiences, recognize destructive patterns, and work toward healthier relational dynamics. This aligns with the journey of personal development, where you strive to overcome challenges, embrace change, and nurture meaningful connections.

Developing Emotional Attunement for Deeper Connections

Cultivating emotional attunement is an essential part of building deeper connections with others. By understanding and responding to the emotional states of those around you, you can create stronger bonds that go beyond surface communication. Emotional attunement requires you to be attentive and sensitive to the emotions of others, recognizing their feelings and validating their experiences. This process involves a conscious effort to tune into the emotional cues expressed through words, body language, or facial expressions, building relationships that are grounded in genuine understanding and empathy.

One effective approach to cultivating emotional attunement is through practicing active listening. In many conversations, people tend to listen passively, often thinking about their replies rather than truly hearing what the other person is saying. By practicing active listening, you demonstrate that you value the speaker's perspective and that you are present in the moment with them.

Empathy plays a pivotal role in emotional attunement as it allows you to recognize and appreciate the emotional experiences of others. Even during disagreements, empathy promotes solidarity by helping individuals feel acknowledged and supported in their feelings. The ability to empathize with someone enables you to bridge differences and build a sense of shared understanding, which reduces conflict and enhances connections.

An additional strategy to enhance emotional attunement involves engaging in discussions where the primary objective is not agreement but understanding. In these instances, participants aim to grasp the emotions driving the other person's words rather than persuading them to change their views. This can be practiced by choosing a topic of conversation where differing opinions exist and then intentionally asking questions to explore and understand the emotional motivations behind each side's stance. By focusing on the underlying emotions rather than the content of the disagreement, you can develop a nuanced appreciation for diverse perspectives, which strengthens empathetic engagement.

Developing emotional attunement requires patience and practice. It is a skill that evolves as you grow more accustomed to acknowledging and appreciating the emotional experiences of those around you. Practicing mindfulness can significantly aid this journey by helping you stay present and focused on your own emotions as well as the emotions of others.

Creating a supportive environment that encourages open emotional expression can enhance emotional attunement. This involves setting aside dedicated time for meaningful conversations where you feel safe expressing your feelings and thoughts with close friends and family. Regularly practicing this kind of intentional interaction helps build trust and comfort, making it easier for you to access and share your emotions freely. An example of this could be family check-ins where each member has an opportunity to share their highs and lows of the week, or evening routine chats where couples discuss their day's events and associated feelings.

For those who find it challenging to achieve emotional attunement independently, seeking professional guidance may be beneficial. Relationship coaches or therapists possess the expertise to guide you and your loved ones through exercises aimed at enhancing emotional connection. Through therapy sessions, you can learn specific techniques to better attune to yourself and others, thereby improving relational dynamics. Professional support can offer valuable insights into personal patterns that might hinder emotional attunement and provide tools to overcome barriers to deeper connection.

Prioritizing Emotional Resilience in All Interactions

Emotional resilience serves as a cornerstone in cultivating emotional safety in relationships. It can be described as the ability to adapt and thrive amidst challenging situations, ensuring that emotional connections remain strong even when faced with adversity (Hurley, 2024). By developing this resilience, you can navigate the ebbs and flows of relationships with grace and understanding, ultimately safeguarding the bond you share with others.

At its core, emotional resilience equips you with the tools to handle stress and emotional upheaval. The reality is that relationships are not immune to challenges; conflicts and misunderstandings are inevitable. During these times, emotional resilience acts as a buffer, allowing you to remain calm and composed instead of succumbing to knee-jerk reactions that may harm the relationship. It's like having an inner anchor that keeps you steady during emotional storms.

One key aspect of building emotional resilience is mastering self-regulation techniques. These methods help manage emotional responses proactively, reducing the likelihood of impulsive emotional exchanges that could escalate conflicts. For instance, taking a moment to breathe deeply before responding to a partner's critical comment can create a pause for reflection rather than overreacting.

Moreover, cultivating a growth mindset significantly contributes to emotional resilience. According to Dr. Carol S. Dweck, a psychologist renowned for her work on mindset, embracing a growth mindset means viewing challenges as opportunities for learning rather than threats to success (Mack, 2023). In a relationship context, this mindset allows individuals to embrace vulnerability and learn from relational experiences, seeing setbacks as stepping stones that have the potential to lead to personal and mutual growth. Instead of fearing failure or conflict, couples with a growth mindset see them as an integral part of deepening their understanding of themselves and their partners.

Another key aspect of emotional resilience is the practice of expressing gratitude and appreciation. Resilient individuals often make it a habit to recognize the positive aspects of their relationships. They might verbally acknowledge their partner's efforts, such as cooking dinner or supporting them during a stressful day. By doing this, they contribute to building a stronger emotional connection.

For example, consider a scenario where one partner takes time out of their day to help the other with a project. A resilient individual would take the moment to say thank you, perhaps acknowledging the specific effort that went into helping. This small act goes a long way in reinforcing feelings of support and validation within the relationship. Over time, these practices form the bedrock of a more positive and harmonious partnership. Practicing emotional resilience transforms the way individuals connect. The approach to conflict resolution, combined with expressions of gratitude, helps in building deeper emotional ties. Partners who regularly engage in these healthy practices often find themselves with a more supportive and understanding relationship.

When partners choose to focus on understanding each other's feelings, they can navigate conflicts with more ease. It can be helpful to set aside time after a disagreement to talk openly about each person's emotional experience. This can take the form of a simple conversation where each partner expresses what they felt during the argument. Through this exchange, each person can work toward understanding the other's perspective.

The positive effects of emotional resilience extend beyond just the individuals involved. Resilience can create a ripple effect that influences family dynamics and interactions with friends. When partners exhibit resilience, they model this behavior to those around them. Children, for instance, learn from their parents. They observe the way conflicts are handled, the importance of gratitude, and the value of emotional awareness.

CHAPTER 7

Furthermore, friendships can benefit from the principles of emotional resilience. When friends confront misunderstandings, resilient individuals may approach the situation with empathy. They often prioritize the relationship over their ego, fostering stronger bonds. Their ability to communicate openly and appreciate their friends' contributions can lead to lasting friendships founded on mutual respect and understanding.

Interactive Exercise

Strengthening Rapport Through Consistent Emotional Presence

Building meaningful, lasting connections requires more than just effective communication. It demands an emotional presence that has the power to establish deep trust and authenticity in relationships. Emotional presence involves being fully engaged and attuned during interactions, which creates a safe and supportive environment. Below are suggestions of simple rituals that you can incorporate in your close relationships (whether with a close friend or your partner) to encourage regular emotional engagement. After practicing each ritual, spend time journaling individually about the experience and what you took away from it.

Rituals for connection:

1. **Daily sharing moments:** Set aside 10–15 minutes each day for participants to share a personal story or experience with a partner. Focus on being present and actively listening without interruptions.

2. **Mindful check-ins:** At the beginning or end of each interaction, take a moment for a mindful check-in. Close your eyes, take a few deep breaths, and ask your partner how they are feeling. Respond with empathy and curiosity.

3. **Gratitude journaling together:** Each week, exchange short notes of gratitude or appreciation for each other. Discuss the notes during a dedicated time to reinforce positive emotional connections.

4. **Shared silence:** Dedicate a few minutes to sit in silence with each other. Use this time to reflect on your individual feelings and the connection you share, enhancing emotional awareness.

5. **The connection jar:** Create a jar filled with prompts or questions related to emotional connection. Take turns drawing a prompt and discussing your thoughts, feelings, and insights.

In your journey through the depths of emotional safety, you've discovered that it's more than just an added layer to communication—it's the essential core for building trust and true connection in relationships. You've learned to go beyond mere words, acknowledging how tones, gestures, and emotional cues function as powerful communicators. By cultivating environments where you and those around you feel secure to expose your genuine selves without fear, you pave pathways to authentic intimacy. Through a lens of empathy, you open up possibilities to understand those closest to you, building bridges not just with words but through shared vulnerabilities and mutual respect.

As we conclude this exploration of emotional safety, remember its profound impact across all types of relationships—from friendships to family bonds and romantic partnerships. When people commit to prioritizing emotional security, they create nurturing spaces leading to growth, healing, and enriched connections. In these realms, there's room to explore differences openly and work through conflicts constructively.

08.

Your Ongoing Journey to Secure Attachment

A healthy relationship is a feast of affection/giving for both people; not one receiving crumbs and trying to convince themselves it's enough. –
Shannon Thomas

Encouraging Ongoing Development of Secure Relationships

Secure attachment is a lifelong journey, an ongoing quest to build stronger, more fulfilling relationships. It's about understanding that your relationships can evolve and flourish when rooted in trust and openness. At times, the path may seem daunting, but the rewards of deeper bonds and self-awareness are worth every step.

Embracing vulnerability emerges as a cornerstone practice for developing secure attachments over time. By allowing yourself to be open and authentic with others, you create space for deeper connections that are rooted in honesty and trust. Vulnerability might feel daunting at first—exposing your fears, dreams, and feelings can seem like risky territory. Yet, it is precisely this openness that lays the foundation for meaningful relationships. When you share your true self, you give others permission to do the same.

Consider a scenario where you decide to open up about a personal challenge with a friend or partner. By sharing your experience, you not only relieve yourself of the burden of carrying it alone but also strengthen your bond with the other person. They gain insight

CHAPTER 8

into your world, possibly resonating with your feelings through shared experiences or understanding. This exchange reinforces the idea that you can rely on each other in times of need. A genuine connection thrives not on perfected facades but on the courage to be vulnerable together.

As we grow, so too must our understanding of relationships. Lifelong learning becomes a crucial component of this process. By committing to continuous learning about human emotions, communication techniques, and relationship dynamics, you remain adaptable and responsive to change. For instance, attending workshops, reading books, or engaging in therapy can provide valuable insights into how to manage your evolving relational needs effectively.

Continuous learning benefits you personally and extends its effects to those around you. It promotes self-discovery by uncovering new aspects of yourself that might previously have been hidden. This newfound self-awareness translates into healthier interactions as you come to understand your needs and preferences better. Moreover, being adaptable allows you to navigate transitions in relationships—such as moving houses, changes in family structures, or job relocations—without compromising your connections.

Sharing personal growth stories can transform your individual achievements into collective empowerment. When you openly discuss your journey toward self-improvement, you create opportunities for mutual support within your social circles. These exchanges act as catalysts for discussions that encourage listening, empathy, and providing constructive feedback. Imagine a situation where you share your enthusiasm for a new skill or hobby that has enhanced your life. Your narrative might inspire your friends or partner to explore new interests, potentially leading to shared activities that further strengthen your bonds.

A community built on shared experiences often finds strength in diversity. Each member contributes unique perspectives, creating a richer understanding and appreciation of one another. This dynamic enhances the resilience of your relationships, as you learn to appreciate different outlooks and grow collectively. In turn, this unity cultivates an environment where everyone feels safe to continue their journey toward greater security and fulfillment in their connections.

Highlighting the Significance of Introspection and Curiosity

Self-reflection and curiosity are essential components in the ongoing journey to achieving secure attachments and personal growth. At its core, this pursuit involves a willingness to explore and understand not only oneself but also the feelings and experiences of others. By embracing curiosity about people's emotions and backgrounds, you open yourself up to greater empathy and deeper connections.

Imagine meeting someone new and genuinely wanting to learn about their life story. This curiosity can break down barriers and create an environment where empathy thrives. When you become curious about what makes others tick, you allow yourself to step into their shoes, even if just for a moment. Such connections are built on understanding and compassion, paving the way for more secure attachments.

Creating safe spaces for open dialogue is equally important in nurturing personal growth and improving relationships. As outlined in the previous chapter, safe spaces are environments where individuals feel comfortable expressing their thoughts and emotions without fear of judgment or ridicule. In these settings, introspection becomes more accessible, and healthy communication flourishes.

Group discussions or therapy settings offer another powerful avenue for exploring attachment styles. Within these groups, individuals are exposed to a variety of perspectives and experiences, which can provide invaluable insights. Hearing others share their challenges and triumphs related to attachment can normalize your own struggles and promote a sense of community. Beyond structured settings, casual gatherings with friends or like-minded individuals can serve as informal group discussions that enrich your understanding of attachment. These are opportunities to engage with diverse outlooks, challenge preconceived notions, and expand your emotional intelligence.

The integration of self-reflection and curiosity in everyday life cannot be overstated. Personal growth is a continual process, and incorporating these practices into daily routines can yield significant benefits over time. Simple actions such as journaling your thoughts, maintaining an openness to feedback, and seeking continuous learning opportunities contribute to a more profound understanding of yourself and others. Through thoughtful self-reflection, you develop a heightened awareness of your strengths and weaknesses. This awareness is crucial when striving for secure attachments, as it encourages accountability and authenticity in your relationships.

Making Room for Setbacks in Your Relationships

When you build strong connections with your loved ones, it can feel like you have everything figured out. However, just because you have formed a secure attachment does not mean your relationships will be free of challenges. In fact, it is quite common to experience setbacks along the way. Life is filled with stressors, triggers, and even new insecurities that can affect how you interact with those you care about.

Sometimes, during tough times, you might realize you are slipping back into old habits that you thought you had overcome. This could happen when you are under pressure at work or dealing with personal issues. For example, if you are feeling overwhelmed, you might start to withdraw from your partner, even if you had previously committed to being more open. It's important to recognize these moments not as failures but as opportunities to grow.

Conversely, there are moments when you feel a sense of distance from your loved ones, even when you are being completely honest and open with them. This can happen in close relationships, like with family or friends, where you both might be going through different experiences that create a gap in your connection. For instance, if your best friend has a new job that takes up a lot of their time, you might feel neglected or left behind, even though they still care for you deeply.

Accepting Setbacks as Normal

Setbacks in a relationship are completely normal. No one is perfect, and expecting perfection from yourself or others can lead to disappointment. When you allow yourself to expect that difficulties will arise, you make room for a healthier perspective. Instead of being hard on yourself or your loved ones, you can look at these challenges as a natural part of the relationship journey.

Making room for setbacks helps you embrace experiences as they come. It is about being open to the fact that relationships can be messy. Trying to hold onto rigid standards often leads to disappointment. Instead, it can be beneficial to take a step back and assess what is really happening. Rather than focusing on the past or being critical of yourself or others, focus on what you can learn from the situation.

For example, if you had an argument with your partner, instead of fixating on the fight itself, think about why it happened. Were there underlying fears or needs that weren't being addressed? Discussing these discoveries calmly can help strengthen the bond between you. It shows that you are willing to navigate through the tough patches together.

The tools you learn in this book can help you work through setbacks. Begin by practicing self-awareness. This means noticing how you feel and identifying any triggers that might cause you to react negatively. Utilize journaling as an effective way to capture your thoughts and feelings. When you write down what you are experiencing, it can help you see patterns in your behavior and responses.

Adjusting Expectations Together

Adjusting expectations is essential when setbacks occur. It is important to check in with your loved ones and recalibrate what you expect from each other. Instead of assuming everything will always be okay or that the other person should know what you need, have conversations to clarify. You might say something like, "I know we've both been busy lately, let's make sure we're still checking in with each other, what do you think?" This reinforces the idea that both parties are responsible for the relationship.

In any relationship, there will always be lessons to learn from each experience, positive or negative. Setbacks do not have to be roadblocks; instead, they can serve as stepping stones for growth. After encountering a challenge, take time to reflect. What worked, what didn't, and what can be improved next time?

It's vital to remember that the goal isn't to avoid all conflicts but rather to learn how to navigate through them more effectively. This continuous learning can lead to stronger bonds. You may find that confronting issues together brings you closer as you build a deeper understanding of one another.

Relationships can have their ups and downs, and that's part of the journey. Embrace each moment as it comes and remember that the ability to grow from setbacks is what makes the bond with your loved ones even more enriching. Learn, adjust, and continue to build connections that can weather any storm.

Final Reflection on Setting Goals in Various Relationships

Goals act as navigational tools, offering clear direction and measurable outcomes in your quest for deeper, more meaningful relationships. When you define personal goals, you essentially create a framework to achieve your relational objectives. This framework can keep you grounded, providing a lens through which you evaluate your interactions and connections with others.

For instance, let's consider someone striving to improve their communication skills within a romantic relationship. Setting a goal to actively listen without interrupting during conversations provides a specific target to aim for. Over time, this repeated action becomes habitual, leading to a smoother exchange of ideas and enhancing the sense of being heard within that relationship. It's not just about listening per se; it's the commitment to consistently strive toward better listening, illustrating how defined goals work in practice.

However, it's crucial to understand that everyone operates within varied environments, each presenting its unique challenges and opportunities. Goal setting in diverse contexts tailors approaches to these specific environments, enhancing their efficacy. For example, while the same individual may have goals for a personal relationship, their professional environment might require different strategies. Here, the focus could shift to becoming more assertive in team meetings, balancing assertiveness with empathy. Such tailored goals respect the nuances of each environment, ensuring that efforts remain relevant and impactful.

Taking a holistic approach allows you to adapt your strategies across different settings—whether at home, work, or within social circles. By doing so, you not only enhance your personal effectiveness but also build a versatile skill set that enriches all areas of your life. This diversity in goal setting requires flexibility and openness to adjust your tactics based on the context.

Celebrating Progress and Adjusting Goals

Achieving goals is undeniably rewarding, yet the real magic happens when you celebrate progress and adjust your goals along the way. Celebrating even small victories instills a sense of pride and accomplishment, reinforcing the effort invested. Whether it's acknowledging a successful week of improved communication or sharing moments when assertiveness opened new doors at work, these celebrations contribute to a positive cycle of encouragement.

Take, for example, the earlier goal of active listening. Once a certain comfort level is reached, it might be time to introduce a new challenge—perhaps learning to ask insightful follow-up questions. By continuously refining and evolving your objectives, you stay engaged and motivated, avoiding stagnation in your progress.

Regularly reviewing and adjusting these goals ensures they remain aligned with your current situation and aspirations. Life is dynamic, constantly providing new insights and experiences that shape who you are and what you seek. In response, your goals should never be static but should evolve alongside you. Checking in on your progress helps maintain focus on individual growth, serving as a reminder of how far you've come and where you wish to go next.

The process of defining, tailoring, celebrating, and adjusting your goals crafts a resilient foundation for nurturing secure attachments. As you navigate through life's various relationships, these structured, flexible strategies guide you toward deeper understanding and connection with yourself and others. Ultimately, cultivating secure attachments through actionable goals transforms not only your relationships but also pushes you toward continuous self-improvement and emotional healing.

Commitment to Adaptability in Evolving Attachmens

Adapting to the shifts in relationships can be as challenging as it is rewarding. When you live in ever-evolving social situations, adaptability becomes a necessity. Thus, you need to recognize change as a constant that allows you to adjust your relationship approaches with flexibility and openness. This mindset prepares you for transitions that are inevitable yet essential for growth. Just like seasons change, so do people and their circumstances, bringing with them opportunities to learn and adapt.

When you anticipate change, you avoid the rigidity that often hampers personal and relational growth. Instead of resisting, embracing change helps you create more resilient relationships. For instance, when you and a romantic partner undergo life changes such as career shifts or parenthood, recognizing these as natural progressions can ease the transition for both of you. You may begin to see these phases as part of a shared journey rather than hurdles to overcome alone. Flexibility becomes the glue that holds your partnership together through thick and thin.

Shared commitment to adaptability strengthens your relational bonds, creating a buffer against adversities. Friends, family, and couples who prioritize adaptability prepare themselves better for unexpected turns, whether they stem from internal dynamics or external pressures. Such resilience acts as a beacon during turbulent times, offering stability and reassurance.

Mutual adaptability, grounded in trust and understanding, can lead to healthier, secure attachments that endure over time. When you and your loved ones embrace adaptability as foundational to your relationships, you inherently promote growth and strengthen your emotional ties. This approach aligns with the natural ebbs and flows of life, making room for individual growth within the context of shared journeys.

SETTING HEALTHY RELATIONSHIP VALUES AND GOALS

_____

_____

_____

_____

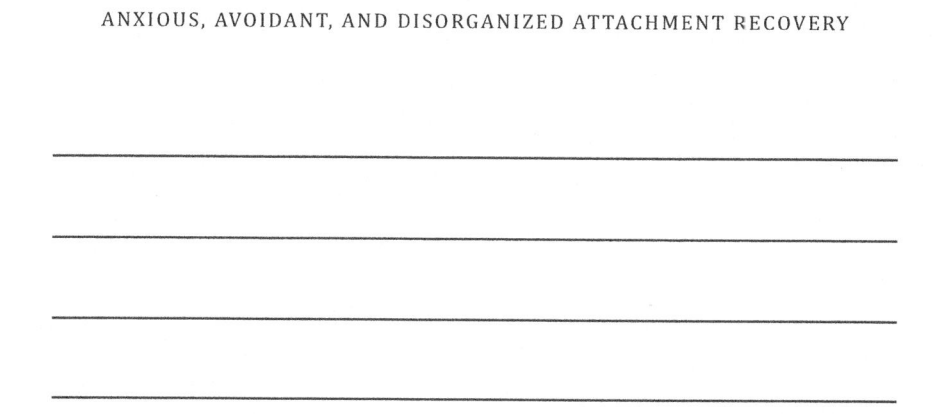

Throughout this chapter, we've explored the importance of strengthening secure attachments in the long term through vulnerability, continuous personal growth, and a commitment to adaptability. By embracing the courage to be open with others, you cultivate trust and intimacy in your relationships. This openness not only strengthens your bonds but also encourages mutual support within your communities.

Such interactions lay the foundation for enduring connections that thrive on authenticity and understanding. In this chapter, you have also looked into practical strategies like setting personal goals, engaging in thoughtful self-reflection, and creating safe spaces for honest communication. These practices enhance your self-awareness over time and contribute to building healthier, more secure relationships.

As we conclude, it's crucial to remember that this journey is ongoing and ever-evolving. Personal growth doesn't happen overnight, nor does achieving secure attachments. It requires patience, dedication, and a willingness to adapt as life's circumstances change. By continuously learning about yourself and others, you become better equipped to navigate the complexities of relationships. Embracing flexibility and resilience empowers you to face challenges with confidence and grace. As you move forward, may these insights guide you toward deeper connections and greater fulfillment in your relational endeavors.

Interactive Exercise

Setting Healthy Relationship Values and Goals

Developing secure attachments with your friends, family, and romantic partners involves understanding shared values and establishing healthy goals. This exercise aims to guide you in identifying what truly matters to you in your relationships and how to nurture them for long-term fulfillment. By clarifying your values and setting achievable goals, you pave the way for deeper connections and a supportive environment where everyone can thrive.

Here are the steps to practice with a loved one:

1. Take a moment to jot down five values that are most important to you in your relationships (e.g., trust, empathy, communication, respect, or honesty). Consider why these values matter and how they influence your connections with others.

2. If you feel comfortable, discuss your identified values with a close friend or family member. Ask them to share their values too and look for common ground. This can help both of you understand each other better.

3. Based on your values, create one to three specific, achievable goals for each type of relationship (friendships, family, or romantic one). For example, a goal for a friendship could be to spend quality time together once a month to strengthen your bond.

4. For each goal, outline the steps you will take to achieve it. Be specific about how you will put your values into practice. For instance, if your goal is to improve communication in a romantic

relationship, consider scheduling regular check-ins to discuss feelings and experiences.

5. Set a reminder to revisit your values and goals every few months. Reflect on the progress you've made and adjust your goals as needed to keep your relationships flourishing.

Conclusion

A healthy relationship keeps the doors and windows wide open. Plenty of air is circulating and no one feels trapped. Relationships thrive in this environment. Keep your doors and windows open. If the person is meant to be in your life, all the open doors and windows in the world, will not make them leave. Trust the truth. –Unknown

Throughout this journey, you have explored the importance of attachment theory. This theory is a way to understand how your early experiences have influenced your relationships. When you were young, your interactions with your caregivers created a framework for how you connected with others later in life. The quality of these connections can be traced to the attachment style you adopted.

Recognizing the types of insecure attachments—whether avoidant, anxious, or disorganized—and understanding their characteristics allows you to confront these challenges with compassion and clarity. This book has taught you that these styles are not fixed destinies but rather starting points for growth and transformation. In other words, through self-awareness and intentional effort, it is possible to unlearn your insecure attachment style and cultivate relationships grounded in security, trust, and mutual respect.

Consider the process of ongoing growth, where nurturing your connections requires commitment and care, much like tending to a garden. Embracing this perspective means acknowledging that developing a secure attachment style is an evolving journey, one that calls for regular self-reflection and adaptability. It's about checking in with yourself and your loved ones consistently, ensuring that the dynamics of your relationships are well-nourished. Acknowledging that both parties will change over time, this endeavor becomes less about achieving perfection and more about engaging with each other openly and honestly.

In assessing your current relationships, it's essential to set specific, actionable goals aimed at building more secure attachments. This could mean initiating weekly check-ins with a partner to discuss needs and feelings, creating a safe space for deeper emotional connection. Within family settings, it might involve practicing active listening to understand the unique perspectives of siblings or parents, thereby bridging generational gaps. In professional spheres, setting boundaries and cultivating open dialogue can enhance coworker relations and minimize conflicts. These tailored goals serve as mile markers on the road to enriching the various relationships in your rich and dynamic life.

The commitment to adaptability remains crucial as you learn to navigate the complexities of evolving relationships. As individuals, we grow and change, and so too must our approach to attachment and connection. Imagine a river flowing through diverse terrains; it teaches us the art of embracing flexibility, seeing changes not as threats, but as opportunities for greater understanding and connection. Navigating differences with this mindset enriches the relational fabric, allowing deeper bonds to form as you move with the natural flow of life.

With each step toward building stronger attachments, remember that transformation isn't something that happens overnight. It requires patience, persistence, and genuine effort. You're cultivating new habits, rewiring patterns of thought that may have been ingrained for years. Celebrate small victories along the way—each represents progress and reflects your dedication to becoming a better version of yourself in the context of your relationships.

Ultimately, the journey to secure attachment serves as a bridge between past experiences and future possibilities. It empowers you to rewrite narratives of insecurity into stories of empowerment and love. In doing so, you lay the foundation for resilient relationships capable of weathering storms and thriving in times of peace. This transformation echoes beyond personal development; it ripples outward, impacting everyone your life touches.

As this book concludes, let it mark not an end, but the beginning of a renewed commitment to personal growth and emotional healing. May you continue to explore attachment theory's concepts, applying them in real-world contexts to cultivate meaningful connections.

POSITIVE SELF-TALK

Although the path may be challenging at times, the rewards—a greater sense of belonging, fulfillment, and joy—are immeasurable.

You are not alone in this endeavor, for many share your quest for profound connection and evolution. Feel free to share your experience of transforming your attachments on the book's Amazon page. Your review can be the confirmation someone needs to take their first step in the life-changing journey of healing their relationship dynamics. Our joint efforts at confronting insecure attachments allow us to build a future where secure, loving relationships flourish, guided by empathy, understanding, and unwavering resolve.

Share Your Experience

Congratulations on completing your journey through the *Anxious, Avoidant, and Disorganized Attachment Recovery Workbook*! Now that you have armed yourself with essential tools to manage your attachment style, it's time to share your newfound wisdom.

By leaving your honest review of this book on Amazon, you're not just offering feedback; you're guiding other readers who are seeking the same transformation. You have the power to direct them to the help they need and to pass along the passion for recovery that this workbook ignites.

Your review plays a crucial role in keeping the life-changing message of the *Anxious, Avoidant, and Disorganized Attachment Recovery Workbook* vibrant and alive. By sharing your experience, you help ensure that others can find this resource and start their own journey of healing and growth.

Thank you for your invaluable contribution. Your support keeps this workbook thriving and continues the cycle of knowledge and healing.

Please, scan the QR code to leave your review:

Together, we're not just reading a book; we're creating a community of awareness, recovery, and mindfulness. Thanks to you, this important work continues. Let's keep the game alive!

With deepest appreciation, Lulu Nicholson

PS - Did you know? Sharing something of value with another person enriches both of your lives. If you believe this book could illuminate someone else's path, consider passing it along.

References

Astray, T. (2020, March 19). Communication tool: Assertive confrontation and boundary setting with the DESO script. Dr. Tatiana Astray. https://www.tatianaastray.com/managing-relationships/2020/3/18/communication-tool-assertive-confrontation-and-boundary-setting-with-the-deso-script

Boundaries III: Communicating boundaries. (2023, October 9). Bullet Journal. https://bulletjournal.com/blogs/bulletjournalist/how-communicating-boundaries-gets-your-needs-met

Brown, B. (2019). Brené Brown quote. Goodreads. https://www.goodreads.com/quotes/823523-when-we-fail-to-set-boundaries-and-hold-people-accountable

Brown McCormick, L. M. (2024, February 19). Polyvagal theory and attachment: Understanding the connection between nervous system regulation and relationships. Women Thrive Counseling. https://www.womenthrivecounseling.com/blog/polyvagal-theory-and-attachment-understanding-the-connection-between-nervous-system-regulation-and-relationships

Channawar, S. N. (2023, December). Mindfulness practices for stress reduction and mental clarity. International Journal of Futuristic Innovation in Arts, Humanities and Management (IJFIAHM), 2(3), 49–59.

Cherry, K. (2023, February 22). What is attachment theory? Verywell Mind. https://www.verywellmind.com/what-is-attachment-theory-2795337

Copley, L. (2024, July 17). Breaking generational trauma with positive psychology. Positive Psychology. https://positivepsychology.com/generational-trauma/#the-fundamentals-of-generational-trauma-explained

Derby, E. (n.d.). Esther Derby quote. In G. Davies. (n.d.). 41 psychological safety quotes and practical directives. Parabol. https://www.parabol.co/resources/psychological-safety-quotes/

Doyle, C., & Cicchetti, D. (2017). From the cradle to the grave: The effect of adverse caregiving environments on attachment and relationships throughout the lifespan. Clinical Psychology: Science and Practice, 24(2), 203–217. https://doi.org/10.1111/cpsp.12192

Emotional intelligence and assertiveness: Communicating needs effectively in conflict situations. (2024, June 19). Ei4Change. https://ei4change.com/emotional-intelligence-and-assertiveness-communicating-needs-effectively-in-conflict-situations/

Georgieva, I., & Georgiev, G. V. (2019). Reconstructing personal stories in virtual reality as a mechanism to recover the self. International Journal of Environmental Research and Public Health, 17(1), 26. https://doi.org/10.3390/ijerph17010026

Heller, D. P. (n.d.). In Hadiah. (n.d.). Best +50 attachment styles quotes. Ineffable Living. https://ineffableliving.com/best-attachment-styles-quotes/

Ho, J. (2024, June 17). What burnout says about your attachment style. Psychology Today. https://www.psychologytoday.com/intl/blog/unlock-your-true-motivation/202406/what-burnout-says-about-your-attachment-style

Hooks, B. (n.d.). Bell Hooks quote. Goodreads. https://www.goodreads.com/quotes/731640-one-of-the-best-guides-to-how-to-be-self-loving

Hurley, K. (2024, July 29). What is resilience? Definition, types, building resiliency, benefits and resources. Everyday Health. https://www.everydayhealth.com/wellness/resilience/

Jethava, V., Kadish, J., Kakonge, L., & Wiseman-Hakes, C. (2022). Early attachment and the development of social communication: A neuropsychological approach. Frontiers in Psychiatry, 13, Article 838950. https://doi.org/10.3389/fpsyt.2022.838950

Johnson, S. (n.d.). Sue Johnson quote. Goodreads. https://www.goodreads.com/quotes/6607748-if-i-appeal-to-you-for-emotional-connection-and-you

Made in the USA
Las Vegas, NV
03 February 2025